PAST and PRESENT

No 69

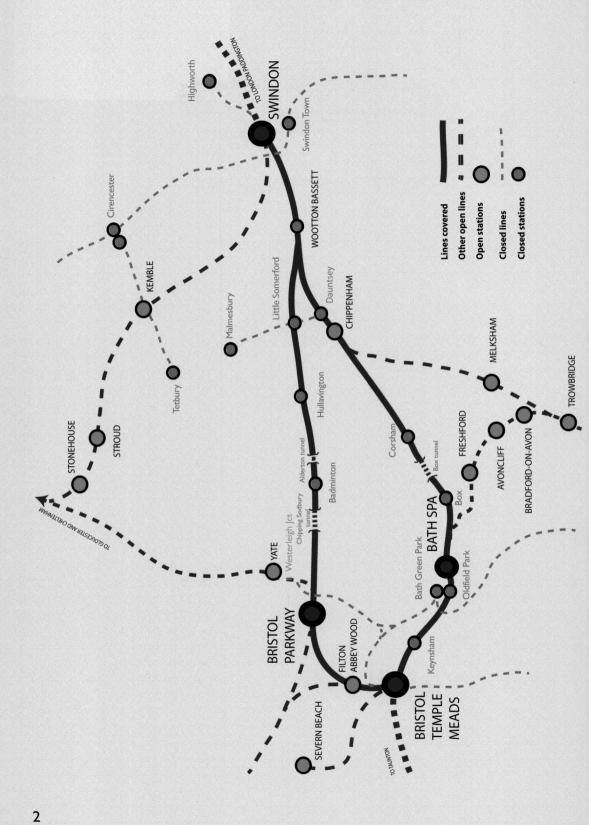

TO LONDON PADDINGTON

Highworth

SWINDON

Swindon Town

Cirencester

WOOTTON BASSETT

KEMBLE

Little Somerford

Dauntsey

CHIPPENHAM

Malmesbury

MELKSHAM

Tetbury

Hullavington

Corsham

FRESHFORD

TROWBRIDGE

STONEHOUSE

STROUD

Alderton tunnel

Badminton

Box tunnel

AVONCLIFF

BRADFORD-ON-AVON

Chipping Sodbury tunnel

Box

BATH SPA

TO GLOUCESTER AND CHELTENHAM

Westerleigh Jct

YATE

Bath Green Park

Oldfield Park

BRISTOL PARKWAY

FILTON

ABBEY WOOD

Keynsham

SEVERN BEACH

BRISTOL TEMPLE MEADS

TO TAUNTON

Lines covered

Other open lines

Open stations

Closed lines

Closed stations

2

BRITISH RAILWAYS

PAST and PRESENT

No 69

Swindon to Bristol

John Stretton and Tim Maddocks

Past & Present • Mortons Books

First published in 2019

British Library Cataloguing in Publication Data

A catalogue record for this book is available from the British Library.

ISBN 978 1 85895 294 9

Past & Present Books
Mortons Media Group Limited
Media Centre
Morton Way
Horncastle
LN9 6JR

Tel/Fax: 01507 529535
email: sohara@mortons.co.uk
Website: www.nostalgiacollection.com

Printed and bound in the Czech Republic

All photographs are by John Stretton unless otherwise credited

ACKNOWLEDGEMENTS

As with any project such as this, there are highs and lows. The latter usually come when you arrive at a promising location to find that the promise is frustrated and/or unfulfilled. The highs, however, are thankfully more frequent, not least from the material submitted by various contributors. There have been gems and the unexpected in the material offered to us. Again, as with the other books that we have prepared, this project would have been so much weaker without these ready and helpful supporters, especially those who have lent us their precious images. So, without hesitation, we thank all who have helped, no matter how small the assistance. It has all been worth it, but deserving of especial mention are Tim Maddocks, for safely completing the mammoth task of researching and writing the captions, and Peter Townsend at Past & Present Publishing, who has believed in us and the project and has played his part in its production, with patience, never failing courtesy and always with encouragement. Like a football team, one needs willing support. Thank you one and all!

SWINDON: On Saturday 9 May 1987, No 6000 *King George V* runs light engine through Swindon station on the Up Main line, prior to working the 'Severn-Wye Express' rail tour, which ran from Hereford to Swindon and back via Severn Tunnel Junction. A couple of Class 47 diesels are visible on the loco stabling point in the background, while a DMU is waiting in Platform 2 to work a local service to Gloucester and Cheltenham via the Stroud Valley. No 6000 spearheaded the 'Return to Steam' on British Rail in 1971, becoming the first locomotive to officially 'break' the notorious steam ban, which had been in place since regular steam operations ended on BR in 1968.

CONTENTS

SWINDON: With light reflecting off the polished side of a London-bound HST service in Platform 3 at Swindon on 5 November 1987, the outlines of the passengers are silhouetted as they board their service. The buildings of Swindon Works can be seen in the background, the facility having been closed by British Rail a mere 19 months earlier, in March 1986. A Class 37 lurks on the former loco stabling siding, which itself would subsequently get swept away when a large (rail-served) steel terminal was built on the site. As we look towards the west and the yellow light of the winter sun, we can also start our journey in that same direction in the pages of this book, as we proceed towards Bristol via both main line routes of the former Great Western Railway.

FOREWORD

by Mark Langman
Network Rail Western Route Managing Director

Time is the relativity of events, without which time has no meaning. Pertinent for a 'past and present' book! 1986 is best known across the globe for humanity stretching the bounds of space as the technology revolution really took hold. We saw the Mir space station launched into our low Earth orbit, as well as the fateful *Challenger* space shuttle disaster.

On firmer soil, it was also the year I joined the railways as a fresh-faced apprentice, ready to start my journey in this exciting industry. My unconditional enthusiasm has not dimmed over the last 33 years, but the context surrounding the railways certainly has changed.

It is hard to believe now, but in 1986 the railways were seen to be in terminal decline. I distinctly remember the run-down and unloved look and feel of the railway. The widespread use of the car, giving people more control over their lives, had seemingly signed the death warrant for Richard Trevithick's creation. Fewer than half the number of people who used Isambard Kingdom Brunel's Great Western Railway in its Victorian heyday were using it in the 1980s.

Closer to the home and theme of this book, the last new-build locomotive rolled off the Swindon Works production line in 1965, a Class 14 shunter, leaving just rolling stock refurbishment work. What was once the largest manufacturing facility in Europe was destined to close on 26 March 1986. There had even been plans put forward to Government to drastically cut the rail network to just the major lines. That would have meant no Trans-Wilts line from Swindon to Westbury and no Golden Valley line to Gloucester and Cheltenham Spa, with the network almost disappearing from Wales and stopping at Plymouth in the south-west peninsula.

That could have been where this Foreword, our story and my career ended. Thankfully those options were never taken up and what we have seen since the 1990s is nothing short of a remarkable railway renaissance. More than double the number of passengers now use trains each year, making them more popular than ever before. The mass transit of goods and people via the railway is vital for the UK's economy — it opens up opportunities for where you want to live, bring up your family, get a job and what you can buy in your local shop.

What we have also seen is a consensus, across the political spectrum, that investing in our national railways is not just right, but essential for the communities and businesses that we serve. In 2017 we saw more investment in upgrading the railway between London Paddington and Cardiff Central than was spent upgrading the entire network between 1955 and 1975. That is an astonishing statistic, but we have not been doing this work out of a fascination with looking at shiny infrastructure. Everything we have done, and continue to do, is for the benefit of our nation, communities, passengers and freight operators.

Sometimes it is some of the smallest schemes that have had the biggest impact. Redoubling 13 miles of railway between Swindon and Kemble may not seem that important, but the much-needed extra capacity enabled the diversion of London to South Wales trains so that we could electrify the Severn Tunnel; and from December 2019 it will mean that Gloucestershire passengers will benefit from hourly services to central London. Also, there has been the 'four-tracking' from Bristol Parkway to Temple Meads and the introduction of IETs.

I cannot even begin to scratch the surface of how much the railway has changed in the last ten years, let alone during my career or the timeframe covered by this book. But I hope you find the history and future of our railways — and this route in particular — as fascinating and exciting as I continue to do every day. Enjoy the read.

INTRODUCTION

This is the third book on which your authors have collaborated, following the 'Past & Present' volumes on the doubling of the two 'Cotswold' lines – *The Cotswold Line* (Worcester-Oxford) and *The Golden Valley Line* (Swindon-Gloucester). The germ of this latest volume originally came from Network Rail, following its appreciation of those two earlier titles, and was due to focus on the transformation of the Great Western main line (GWML) from diesel to electric power. As is now only too widely known, turning Brunel's 'billiard table' into an electric railway has been fraught with problems and delays. The idea for this book, however, has never really left your two authors, so here we are with the finished product.

Its incarnation is different from that originally envisaged, due to the delays and piecemeal nature of the various individual GWML upgrade projects, but we have still tried to encapsulate the 'progress' achieved so far. The state of play in the current railway has meant that we have detoured slightly from a strict 'then' and 'now' format, but without losing either the general theme of comparative views or the narrative of the route over a longer period. We hope you will understand and still enjoy the fare presented within the pages.

In steam days, both Swindon and Bristol and the lines between were a very special places for railway enthusiasts. Swindon was graced with a sizeable locomotive depot and extensive railway works, and Bristol was served by three large engine sheds, a major joint passenger station and a network of goods and dock lines. With healthy allocations, a bewildering array of motive power and varied types of train workings, both locations became a Mecca for enthusiasts, historians and photographers. It is to these latter heroes that we owe an enormous debt generally but, as regards this volume, we could not have told the story so well without their efforts.

Being a third volume from your authors, it has given us the opportunity to trawl for fresh shots and we have been fortunate to come up with many that, as far as we are aware, have not been seen

SWINDON: Four diesel locos, of what we might now term 'heritage' design, stand on the loco stabling sidings just to the west of Swindon station on Friday 14 July 1995. Nos 37057, 37098, 58015 and an unidentified third Class 37 might normally be expected to be out working on a weekday, but this was during the first (of two) national ASLEF one-day strikes of that year. The threat of further strikes was lifted on 10 August, following negotiations whereby British Rail improved its offer covering pay and working hours. The fact that three of the locomotives in this picture are carrying different liveries reflects the disaggregation of British Rail's freight business into several different sub-sectors prior to eventual privatisation.

in print before. The book has also benefitted greatly from our own personal experiences, not least, in many cases, being on site with the 'men and machines' to capture views not widely seen by a wider public. We were especially blessed to have been given access to Box Tunnel during the pre-electrification works. Walking the 2 miles of Brunel's creation was truly an experience to be remembered!

Steam and much else besides has disappeared from the route over the years but, thankfully, farsighted cameramen recorded much that was around prior to this, which now gives us both pleasure and a hankering for days gone by. Sadly, our present railway is often so much poorer in aesthetics, especially where infrastructure and signalling are concerned, but with the proliferation of liveries and new types of motive power over the years there is at least some variety still to be had. The railway may be much changed, but for the photographer there is still much to capture, with the challenge now even greater than of yore to create a satisfying image! It would be wonderful to see some stations and/ or lines re-open, but this is 'pie in the sky' and wishful thinking in most instances — however, one can but dream! And there is a message there for our present-day photographers — the future will need the images that you could take today!

SWINDON: the original Down platform and all of the associated steam age infrastructure is still extant in this view taken on 4 April 1946, with No 2927 *Saint Patrick* at the head of a Down working, the headlamps telling us that this was an express service. This loco entered traffic in 1907 and was to give a total of 44 years of service, before being withdrawn in December 1951. No 2920 *Saint David* was the last of this graceful class to be withdrawn from service, and sadly all the original locomotives were scrapped. An interesting but seemingly little-known fact is that No 2937 *Clevedon Court* almost made it into preservation following withdrawal in 1953, as it was to be purchased from BR with the intention of being displayed at the stately home of the same name. An attempt was even made to deliver the locomotive to its new home, but incredibly the engine was returned to Swindon for scrapping because the lorry carrying it was unable to negotiate the driveway up to the house! This gap in the ranks of preserved GW locos has finally been filled, with the official unveiling of No 2999 *Lady of Legend* at the Didcot Railway Centre in April 2019, the culmination of a 15-year project to build a 'Saint' Class loco using a number of key parts from No 4942 *Maindy Hall* as the basis of the work, together with many 'new-build' components. *H. C. Casserley*

Swindon to Wootton Bassett

SWINDON: British Railways Standard Class 4 4-6-0 No 75000 stands in the Down bay, Platform 2, at the west end of Swindon station on 15 April 1956, with the REC 'Severn Venturer' rail tour. 'Castle' Class No 5051 *Earl Bathurst* (formerly *Drysllwyn Castle* until 1937) stands in Platform 4 with the 9.55am Paddington to South Wales excursion. The 'Severn Venturer' itself had started at Paddington and continued on from Swindon to cross the former Severn railway bridge and visit branch lines in the Forest of Dean and Gloucestershire, before returning to Paddington. *Earl Bathurst* is now preserved by the Great Western Society at Didcot and has worked on the main line since restoration, although at the time of writing is currently 'out of ticket'. The entire Down-side island platform and associated bay platforms at Swindon station were taken out of use in 1968, when the Swindon station area was resignalled with multiple aspect signalling controlled from a new panel signal box, located on the Down, London, side of the station. This in turn has also now been swept away (although the internal operating panel has been preserved) and replaced by a large 'Route Operations Centre' (contemporary parlance for a 'mega-signal box'), which opened on an industrial estate near the railway at Didcot in 2010. *Frank Hornby*

SWINDON: On 4 April 1946 No 5001 *Llandovery Castle* is seen passing through Swindon at the head of a Down working. The stock for a Down train waits in Platform 4, having been brought into the station by 'Bulldog' 4-4-0 No 3421, one of the passenger pilots.

How times change! In virtually the same spot as *Llandovery Castle*, No 47345 is seen passing Swindon on the Down Main line with 4V16, the 0945 Southampton-Cardiff Freightliner service on 9 January 1998. The remnant of the old Platform 4 line is still in use to the right of the train, serving the former parcels platform, which can just be glimpsed in the middle distance. The silver-clad building of Swindon Panel Signal Box can be seen to the right of the parcels canopy. Following the demolition of the former Down-side island platform, a large office block now occupies the site (this building is now known as 'Signal Point'), together with an access road to the large car park built on the site of the former carriage works on the Down side of the line to the west of the station. *H. C. Casserley/MJS*

SWINDON: This further photograph dated 4 April 1946 was seemingly taken only a few minutes before or after that featuring *Llandovery Castle*. Note that while the Down Main starting signal is cleared, the distant arm under it remains at 'caution'. Of interest to modellers is the ash pit at the end of Platform 4 and the ATC ramp immediately ahead of the signal on the Down Main.

We now fast-forward almost to the present day. On 19 January 2016 No 43132 draws into the new Platform 4 with 1C13, the 1200 London Paddington to Bristol Temple Meads express. Just like *Llandovery Castle* and No 47345, the train is running on the Down Main line. The new Platform 4, which was built on the course of the former parcels line, was opened in 2003 to overcome operational delays inherent in the 1968 track layout, whereby Down trains had to cross the Up line to gain access to the passenger station. *H. C. Casserley/MJS*

SWINDON: We are now right up to date as we view Swindon station from almost the same vantage point as the previous pictures, as an unidentified Class 800 InterCity Express Train arrives in Platform 4 on 8 November 2018 forming the 1500 Paddington to Bristol service. The unmistakeable silhouettes of the recently commissioned 25kV overhead line equipment dominate the scene, the power having been officially switched on as of 28 June 2018. The train will complete the journey from Swindon to Bristol Temple Meads in 'diesel mode', as the electrification beyond Chippenham towards Bath Spa and Bristol Temple Meads had been 'indefinitely deferred' by the Government in November 2016, due to escalating project costs.

Paul Stanford

SWINDON: On 22 September 1980 an early evening Down train worked by an unidentified Class 31 loco stands in Platform 3. The leading vehicle is a BR Mark I 'BG' Full Brake, which is probably conveying parcels or mail traffic. This eminently sensible use of the railway system ended in January 2004, following a decision by Royal Mail to stop using trains to convey mail. With this decision the last of the Travelling Post Office trains was withdrawn, thus ending a practice that dated back almost to the very beginning of railways in this country. Such is progress. That was not the end, though, because Royal Mail subsequently resumed the conveyance of some pre-sorted mail on a very limited number of routes.

On Monday 9 December 2013 the same viewpoint offers a somewhat neater and tidier platform, as 1A13, the 1030 Bristol Temple Meads to Paddington HST service, stands in Platform 3, doing its station work. Power car No 43063 looks in almost 'ex-works' condition as the train waits for the 'right away'. By this time, most Down trains would be using Platform 4, leaving Platforms 1 and 3 available for their original purpose, the handling of Up services. It should be pointed out, however, that in common with most modern track layouts, all current through platforms at Swindon are signalled for bi-directional movements, thus ensuring maximum operational flexibility at times of disruption. *Tom Heavyside/MJS*

SWINDON: We move a little eastward along Platform 3 on the same date as the previous picture in order to get a better view of the new Down platform, opened in 2003. Power car No 43012 leads 1B22, the 1015 Paddington to Cardiff service, into the station. The provision of this platform on the Down Main line itself has brought about significant train performance improvements to this section of the Great Western main line, because not only are Down trains no longer at the 'whim' of delayed up services, but they can also implement a more efficient braking and acceleration pattern.

SWINDON: This almost 'traditional' sight would soon change. Power car No 43150 stands in Platform 3 on Tuesday 17 September 2015, forming the rear of 1L55, the 1128 Swansea-Paddington service, while on the right in Platform 4 No 43133 is the leading power car working 1C14, the 1230 Paddington-Bristol Temple Meads service. This view illustrates well the generally clean and tidy condition in which the FGW/GWR HST sets were kept towards the end of their service with that operator.

SWINDON: Swindon Station West Signal Box shares 'centre stage' in this view looking west with 'Castle' Class 4-6-0 No 5093 *Upton Castle*, which is arriving at Platform 5 with a train from Cardiff on 28 June 1956. To the right of the train a Hawksworth '94XX' pannier tank appears to be at a stand to enable some staff on the ground to speak to the footplate crew. The extensive carriage works and associated sidings can be seen on the left of the picture, and the even larger locomotive works to the right of the arriving 'Castle'. What a superb photograph like this also shows us is the sheer complexity and proliferation of the steam-age infrastructure, a source of delight for historians and model railway enthusiasts but doubtless a nightmare for the 'bean counters'!

In very wintery conditions on 1 February 2019, No 66541 eases a Wentloog to Southampton Freightliner service into the Through line at Swindon station, possibly to be recessed there for an Up passenger service to pass. The contrast with the 1956 view could not be more complete, although the recently installed overhead line equipment still makes for a fairly 'busy' view, infrastructure-wise. The site of the former carriage works is now a large car park for rail users. Some of the remaining buildings of the former locomotive works can just be made out in the right background. *Mike Timms/Paul Stanford*

SWINDON: Still wearing a faded livery of red and dark grey, EWS-owned No 08757 shunts a rake of empty JXA and POA scrap wagons off the main lines and into Swindon station on 28 June 2004. The Hawksworth steel terminal, which opened in 2008, is located just behind the train, the access line for which can be seen to the right of the '08'.

SWINDON STATION WEST: On 5 October 1965 No D0280 *Falcon* departs from Platform 5 with a Down express from Paddington to Bristol Temple Meads. The experimental *Falcon* was built by Brush at Loughborough and started trials with British Railways Eastern Region in September 1961. By 1965 it had been reallocated to Bath Road to work passenger diagrams between Bristol and Paddington. No further locomotives of this type were constructed because diesel locomotive design had already advanced sufficiently quickly to render it almost obsolete. It did bear a more than passing resemblance to the Brush Type 4 diesel-electric loco, though, later to become the ubiquitous Class 47.

By early 2016 the resignalling of the Western Region had advanced as far westwards as Rushey Platt, just to the west of Swindon, meaning that the lines through Swindon station were now controlled by the Thames Valley Signalling Centre in Didcot. The last train to be signalled through Swindon station by the old panel was 1C36, the 2230 FGW HST service from Paddington to Cardiff Central on the night of Friday 20 November 2015. A weekend possession then followed, with trains on the Monday morning coming under the control of the new signalling positions at Didcot. On Tuesday 19 January 2016 the new signals at the west end of Swindon station frame No 66701 as it passes under the new gantry with 6M40, the 1156 Westbury to Cliff Hill. The main reason for resignalling the GWML, apart from the fact that the old 1968 signalling was essentially life-expired, was to provide compliant, immunised signalling for the forthcoming electrification works.
Ben Ashworth/MJS

SWINDON STATION WEST: Just a few days after the view of *Falcon* departing towards Bristol, on Saturday 9 October 1965 No D1732 arrives with an Up express to Paddington, composed of BR Mark 1 stock in maroon livery. The signal box would have another three years of active service before the advent of multiple aspect signalling.

Almost 40 years of change can be seen in this comparative view taken on 11 December 2004, as 'King' Class 4-6-0 No 6024 *King Edward I* accelerates Past Times' 'The Merchant Venturer' rail tour along the Up Relief line, following a water stop adjacent to the former locomotive works in the background. Although the train started and terminated at Taunton, the 'King' worked between Bristol Temple Meads and Paddington and return. *Tom Heavyside/MJS*

SWINDON WEST: On 9 January 1998 No 37686 approaches Swindon station with a train of empty ZKV and ZCV wagons for Cocklebury Yard, just to the east of the station. The 26-ton vacuum-fitted ZKV wagons (previously coded MSV in TOPS) were formerly used to convey aggregates in commercial traffic, but were transferred to the Departmental fleet in the 1980s and recoded ZKV. Some old PW men anecdotally referred to the ZKV as the ideal spoil wagon because of its high capacity relative to its length, together with the fact that 'the sides were tall enough that the guard couldn't see how much had been put in them!'

In a view taken just a few yards further towards the station, five-car 'Adelante' Class 180 unit No 180101 approaches on the Relief line with an unidentified empty stock working. Fourteen of these units were built by Alstom for FGW and were introduced into passenger service in December 2001. Interestingly for a unit designed and built for services on the 'Western', these units are technically diesel-hydraulics. FGW dispensed with their services in 2009 and they were redeployed elsewhere in the country by Angel Trains with other TOCs, but from the summer of 2012 FGW took five of the sets back into service, mainly for use on the 'Cotswold' line again.

SWINDON WORKS: This fascinating photograph taken in 'A' Shop in October 1933 shows several Collett '48XX' 0-4-2Ts under construction, with Nos 4823 and 4824 closest to the camera. The '48XX' series would later be renumbered as '14XX', which is the label by which this class of locomotive is perhaps best known by enthusiasts. A total of 75 examples were built between 1932 and 1936. A further 20 examples of the virtually identical but non-auto-fitted '58XX' Class were also built. Four examples of the '14XX' Class have been preserved. *MJS collection*

SWINDON WORKS: On 13 February 1994 a couple of 'mock-ups' of retail units for the proposed Retail Outlet Village, which would be subsequently built on part of the works site, appear to mock the proud industrial history of this once substantial engineering site. Some old track is still extant but sadly the magnificent 'A' Shop would not survive, eventually being demolished to make way for a housing estate. Other parts of the works were more fortunate, having listed status. Part of the site was indeed given over to retail use as the 'Designer Outlet Village', while other buildings now see use as offices and other commercial premises. To railway enthusiasts, however, the best-known use of the site is probably the STEAM railway museum, appropriately dedicated to all aspects of the Great Western Railway.

SWINDON WORKS: An icon of the Great Western Railway is seen in a familiar yet incongruous setting. On 10 February 1997 4-4-0 No 3440 *City of Truro* has been positioned within the new 'Retail Outlet Village'. It will not be working a train any time soon, but rather is to become a mere railway-themed backdrop to the new cafe complex. Tables and chairs were subsequently placed alongside the locomotive, which would soon face the ignominy of having empty latte cups placed on its running plate! *City of Truro* was later replaced by No 4930 *Hagley Hall*.

WOOTTON BASSETT: Class 47/4 No 47627 *City of Oxford* approaches Wootton Bassett on 25 March 1987 with empty rubbish containers from Calvert, destined for the three waste transfer facilities in the Bristol/Bath area at Bath Goods, Bristol Barrow Road and Westerleigh Yard. All were operated by different local authorities but used the same rail operation to move waste from the area to a landfill site at Calvert, Buckinghamshire. The changing economics surrounding waste disposal and recycling mean that none of these waste transfer stations is now operational.
Brian Morrison

WOOTTON BASSETT JUNCTION: This view, looking west, dates from 22 September 1980 and shows HST set No 253001, still in the original HST InterCity livery, forming an unidentified Up working. Careful examination of the photograph shows the junction to be set for the Badminton line, so this will be a service from Cardiff or Swansea to Paddington. The Badminton route, which was opened in 1903, diverges to the right behind the rear power car and is hidden by the trees. The original GWR main line route via Box to Bath and Bristol runs straight on, via the elegant three-arch stone bridge in the distance. Note the rail-served terminal for stone from the Mendip quarries of Whatley and Merehead on the left, which is still receiving aggregates by rail from the Somerset quarries today.

On 25 August 2006, the last day of services before a nine-day possession to completely relay the junction, 1A19, the 1330 Bristol Temple Meads to Paddington service, passes clear of the junction points with No 43098 leading. The track layout at the junction is the same as that 26 years earlier but the lineside vegetation has been allowed to grow, with the result that the Mendip stone terminal to the left of the main lines is now obscured from view. *Tom Heavyside/MJS*

WOOTTON BASSETT JUNCTION: On 25 August 2006 some of the new track for the relaying of the junction is laid out, ready for installation. The main lines and Up Goods Loop can be seen to the left of the blue safety fence, while the junction itself is just beyond the brick building in the distance. The new pointwork was configured to maintain the diverging junction line speed of 70mph towards Badminton.

The second picture is a general view of the junction taken on the same day, looking westwards towards Box and Badminton.

WOOTTON BASSETT JUNCTION: Our view shifts slightly to the left and, two days after the previous view on 27 August, some of the old junction track has been removed prior to the replacement fittings being installed. The nearer road-rail machine is standing on the Down Main line, with the further machine on the Up Main. The Up Goods Loop has also been truncated, to allow the installation of the new pointwork that will connect it to the Up Main at the east end of the site. Of interest to rail industry people is that at this date (2006), the wearing of 'full orange' high-visibility clothing was not yet mandatory.

WOOTTON BASSETT JUNCTION: On 29 August 2006 No 66209 stands within the worksite on the Down Main, awaiting permission to move its engineering train in accordance with the requirements of the site Engineering Supervisor. All such movements are made at extremely slow speed and are normally controlled by radio communications. The yellow numerical signs are in connection with temporary speed restrictions applying to the site, following eventual hand-back to traffic.

WOOTTON BASSETT JUNCTION: This very interesting view of the junction was taken in 1921, looking eastwards from the embankment above the Down Badminton line. The five lines of railway in the left foreground are, from left to right, the two Up Goods Loops, the Up Badminton, the Down Badminton and the Down Goods Loop. The path in the foreground leads to Wootton Bassett West signal box, which sits in the vee of the junction. Note the single slip in the Up Badminton line, allowing access to the Down Badminton line from the distant goods yard beyond the junction. An interesting array of signals and other infrastructure is on display, together with some old four-wheeled passenger stock and goods vehicles in the Down sidings. This view would not be available today, due to the amount of vegetation growth. *R. M. Casserley collection*

Badminton to Stoke Gifford

LITTLE SOMERFORD station was the first passing place west of Wootton Bassett, with Up and Down platform loops provided for stopping passenger and goods services to be looped for faster trains to pass. In this view taken on 9 July 1959, looking towards London, a small tank locomotive appears to be the motive power for the short goods train in the Up Platform loop. This may indicate that this was a working from Malmesbury, rather than a local pick-up goods, calling at all stations

along the main line. Little Somerford became a junction in 1933, when the Dauntsey to Malmesbury branch, which formerly ran underneath the Wootton Bassett to Stoke Gifford line, was physically joined by means of a London-facing junction to the west of Little Somerford station. All services on the Dauntsey to Little Somerford section were later withdrawn, although much of the branch was retained as wagon storage for many years. The Malmesbury passenger service was an early casualty of British Railways, being withdrawn in September 1951, although goods services continued to run until 1962. *H. C. Casserley*

HULLAVINGTON: This was the next station beyond Little Somerford, although no passing loops were provided here until 1941, when both the Up and Down Refuge sidings were converted to loops. This view was also taken on 9 July 1959 and shows the station looking towards Stoke Gifford and South Wales. A small goods yard was provided on the Up side of the line, opposite the signal box. Closure to passengers came in April 1961, although the goods yard remained open until October 1965 and the signal box until 1968, when signalling control was transferred to the then new Swindon Panel signal box. The Up and Down loops remain in use to this day, although they are now controlled from the Thames Valley Signalling Centre at Didcot. *R. M. Casserley*

BADMINTON: This view, looking towards Swindon, was taken on the same day. The 61-lever signal box can be glimpsed beyond the Down-side station buildings, under the canopy, opposite which is the well-used goods yard. Traffic at this station was busier than at others along the line, especially in connection with the Beaufort Hunt, and it was not unusual for special trains to be run to Badminton as a result. Despite the other local stations on the line closing to passengers in April 1961, objections from the Duke of Beaufort ensured that Badminton remained open for a few years longer, retaining a number of direct services to and from London Paddington. These remaining passenger services outlasted the goods facilities, which were closed in November 1966. *R. M. Casserley*

BADMINTON: This was the most important station on the Wootton Bassett to Stoke Gifford route and was located exactly 100 miles from Paddington. The station was opened, together with the rest of the route, on 1 July 1903 and took its name from the nearby country seat of the Duke of Beaufort, together with the villages of Great and Little Badminton. This is the Down-side approach road on 9 July 1959, with a variety of vintage motor vehicles parked next to the station buildings. The station was still fully open at this time and the whole scene looks well cared for. *H. C. Casserley*

Above: **Except for Badminton, all the stations shown here are happily still with us. Back in 1965, however, Badminton station still had a few more years of life left and one could travel (Second Class) to London Paddington and back for the princely sum of 29 shillings (£1.45 in decimal currency). If only that were still possible now!** *David Holmes*

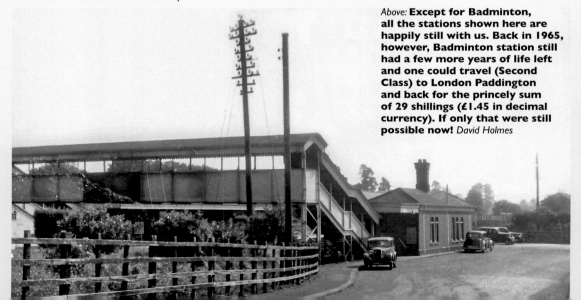

BADMINTON: The station is seen here on 21 September 1968, looking towards South Wales. It had finally closed to passenger services on 3 June of that year, so this unidentified DMU working is either an enthusiasts' special or possibly an official 'inspection special'. The signalling was still operational here following the withdrawal of passenger services, the signal box not closing until May 1971, when control of the area was transferred to Bristol Panel. All loops and points at Badminton were decommissioned from that time and subsequently removed, with just the plain line of the Up and Down lines remaining.

No 66068 is captured at Badminton on Sunday 22 August 2010, with an engineer's train of empty and spoilt ballast wagons, during a further possession for work in and around Chipping Sodbury Tunnel. This telephoto view was taken from the site of the Down platform at Badminton station; the girder bridge carrying the Badminton to Acton Turville road is common to both views. During a number of blockades in the summer of 2017, with train diversions in place, Network Rail installed the overhead line equipment (OLE) in both Alderton and Chipping Sodbury tunnels. Within the approximate 550 yards of Alderton Tunnel conventional OLE was installed, whereas for technical reasons a solid conductor rail was hung above the tracks within the longer Chipping Sodbury Tunnel.
Colour-Rail collection/MJS

CHIPPING SODBURY: We have now passed through Chipping Sodbury Tunnel, some 2½ miles in length under the southern flank of the Cotswold Ridge, to reach the site of Chipping Sodbury station. In this view looking towards Bristol Parkway and South Wales, taken on 1 March 1985, No 6024 *King Edward I* is running at speed past the former Up platform and goods shed with a charter train from Swansea. The loco had previously worked from Newton Abbot to Swansea a few days previously on 25 February with the 'Exe-Tawe' charter train. Photographers are spread about all over the operational infrastructure. Your authors recall that this wasn't even acceptable to Railtrack management back then, so one can only assume that the local operations staff and the British Transport Police were elsewhere. *Ben Ashworth*

CHIPPING SODBURY: The passage of some 25 years has seen changes at Chipping Sodbury. In this view, looking east back towards the tunnel in the distance, the 0815 Paddington to Cardiff Central service passes the site of the old station on 1 September 2010. The old goods shed was finally demolished a few years after the photograph of *King Edward I* was taken and the siding into it lifted, but the other remaining siding in the former goods yard is still extant and remains in use for the stabling of tampers and other on-track machines to this day. The former Up platform has been demolished but the Up Goods Loop (formerly the Up Platform Loop) remains in use. Part of the 'lagoon', used to accommodate flood water pumped out of Chipping Sodbury Tunnel during very wet weather, can be seen at the back of the former goods yard.

WESTERLEIGH WEST JUNCTION: On 14 August 1965 Hawksworth 'Modified Hall' No 7908 *Henshall Hall* approaches the junction with 1M34, the 1005 (Saturdays only) from Kingswear to Wolverhampton Low Level composed of what appears to be Stanier coaching stock. The double track of the former Midland Railway main line can be seen passing beneath the GW line; this was normally the main route for most trains running northwards from Bristol Temple Meads and beyond until its closure in January 1970.

In the second view the cameraman turns his lens 180 degrees to catch the same train as it proceeds round the curve towards Westerleigh North Junction and Yate. The Badminton lines pass in front of the signal box. The earthworks for the east curve from Westerleigh North to East junctions can be seen in the distance above the train. *Both Ben Ashworth*

COALPIT HEATH was the next station west of Chipping Sodbury and is seen here, looking towards Westerleigh Junction and Swindon, on 10 December 1946. The rake of wooden-bodied coal wagons in the distance is probably stabled there in connection with traffic from the local collieries at Frog Lane and Mayshill, both of which were connected to the Up side of the Badminton route a little to the east of Coalpit Heath station. There was also a connection to New Engine Yard, the terminus of a freight-only branch off the Midland main line, which passed under the GW line a little further east. Note the station master's house to the right of the Down-side station building. *R. M. Casserley collection*

COALPIT HEATH: Near the site of Coalpit Heath station, No 220016 accelerates away from the Bristol Parkway station stop on 22 August 2010 forming the 0925 Plymouth-Newcastle CrossCountry service. It is perhaps sobering to reflect that these modern-looking trains are in fact almost 20 years old now. Such a service would at one time have been composed of rather more loco-hauled coaches, running via the former Midland main line via Mangotsfield, albeit at a considerably lower frequency than the present-day service, which offers trains to the Midlands and the north every half-hour. The opening of Bristol Parkway station on 1 July 1972 was almost certainly being considered by British Rail at the time that the Mangotsfield route was closed, and the phenomenal growth of the new station has meant that there is now a considerable commercial advantage in all CrossCountry services calling there.

BRISTOL PARKWAY/
STOKE GIFFORD EAST:

In this pre-electrification view of the approaches to Bristol Parkway taken on 22 August 2010, much has already changed from the initial, basic station that was opened in 1972. The new Up Platform 4, which was opened in 2007, can be seen to the right of the two main through lines. The Up Goods Loop is the next line to the right of Platform 4, with the Network Rail Training Centre to the right of that, accessed via the right-hand divergence of the tandem turnout in the middle of the picture. The Training Centre was opened in 2008, on the site of the former rail-served Royal

Mail terminal, which despite having only been opened in 2000, was closed in 2004 after a scandalously short working life, due to the Royal Mail's regrettable decision to withdraw from rail transport. An unidentified four-car 'Voyager' set approaches the station forming the 1212 Birmingham New Street to Plymouth service. To the left of the CrossCountry train is the Down Goods Loop, from which the Down Reception line diverges in the middle distance. The remaining sidings of Stoke Gifford Down Yard can be seen to the left of that, currently leased and operated by Freightliner Heavy Haul.

The present-day scene is now very different from that of 2010, with a profusion of robust electrification infrastructure readily apparent. No 158766 leaves Bristol Parkway on Tuesday 7 August 2018 forming 2M97, the 0823 Southampton Central to Great Malvern semi-fast service. The former Down Goods Loop has now been designated a through passenger line, with the opening of the fourth platform at Bristol Parkway (paradoxically designated as 'Platform 1'). Although a considerable amount of relaying has been done in recent years, it is interesting and perhaps unfortunate that the turnout from what is now the Down Platform Loop line into the Down Goods Loop (former Down Reception) is still designed for a mere 15mph. In operational terms this can be somewhat restrictive, as lengthy freight services will take additional time to clear the main line.

BRISTOL PARKWAY: The extent of the facilities (or lack of them) available to prospective passengers is seen here in this superb image of the station from the Up side, taken in the year that it opened, 1972. The surface of the former Stoke Gifford Up Yard (left) seems to be some kind of rough gravel. The original, very basic station building is seen here. Due to the presence of the two Up Goods loops, both platforms could only be accessed via the footbridge. A wonderful selection of period cars is on display. *Neil Avent collection*

BRISTOL PARKWAY: In another image from the early days of the station, also taken in 1972, a typical express train of the period is seen, probably destined for Cardiff or Swansea, formed with Mark I coaches in the Corporate blue and grey livery, undertaking its station work in the Down platform. The remains of Stoke Gifford Down Yard appear fairly busy, with a rake of 'Presflo' cement wagons prominent, no doubt destined for the terminal in Lawrence Hill goods yard or Avonside Wharf. There's also a VAA box van visible, possibly conveying Guinness traffic for Kingsland Road Sidings near Bristol East Junction. The HTV or HTO coal hoppers at the back may be destined for either Filton Junction Coal Concentration Depot, which closed in 1991, or Wapping Wharf, which closed in 1987. *Neil Avent collection*

BRISTOL PARKWAY: On 13 May 1992 power car No 43128 heads a Down working approaching the station. The set in the adjacent Down Goods Loop arrived there from the Swindon direction and returned back towards Swindon approximately 30 minutes later, possibly on a test run or in connection with driver training.

Under threatening clouds No 60092 approaches on the Down Main line on Saturday 9 April 2016 with the 1125 Theale (Murco) to Robeston oil train. Although not yet in use, new signals have been installed in readiness for electrification. The rear of the Up Platform Loop (Platform 4) can be seen on the left, with the area immediately to the right of the locomotive being that soon to be occupied by the new Down Platform 1. *Jon Stubley/MJS*

BRISTOL PARKWAY: Looking back in time to 5 May 1982, with No 47022 passing through the station with the empty stock of the High-Speed Track Recording Unit, we can see how much the station has been developed and improved over the years. At the time this photograph was taken it had been open a mere ten years and still appears rather spartan when compared with the facilities available today. There are just two platforms, of course, but at least these now have canopies. The 'bus shelter' facilities are unheated and very basic. Note the absence of the present-day additional storey on the large car park, built on the site of the former Stoke Gifford Up Yard.

The prospects for the intending traveller appear much improved on 22 August 2010, as HST power car No 43125 forms the rear of a passenger service reversing out of the station to run via Filton Bank and Bath Spa to London, due to engineering works to the east of Westerleigh Junction. The new Up Platform 4 is now in use and the commodious new station building, opened in 2001 with significantly enhanced passenger facilities, can be seen above the cab of the HST power car. Unfortunately for the passengers travelling to London on this train, it was to sustain further delay at Stapleton Road, due to a signal failure! The restoration of four tracks between Filton Junction and Dr Days Bridge Junction in 2018 has reduced the risk of this kind of incident causing delay in the future. *Tom Heavyside/MJS*

BRISTOL PARKWAY: The first electric train from Paddington to Bristol Parkway ran on electric power throughout on 31st December 2018, and public services started on 2 January 2019. On 6 February 2019 nine-car IET No 800306 has just arrived from London. Due to the fact that the electrification beyond Bristol Parkway to Cardiff had not yet been commissioned, the pantograph has already been lowered, prior to the rest of the journey being made under diesel power. Since electric power was switched on as far as Bristol Parkway, some trains have been making up 2 or 3 minutes on current Working Timetable timings, which has improved GWR's performance statistics. The final piece of electrification from Bristol Parkway to Cardiff Central is due to be commissioned in December 2019. Set No 800306 was named after Lance-Corporal Allan Leonard Lewis VC and Flight Sub-Lieutenant Harold Day DSC just prior to Remembrance Sunday in November 2018, in honour of the two First World War heroes. The set also honours more than 2,500 workers of the old Great Western company, who also gave their lives in the conflict and whose names are also depicted in panels along the length of the new electric set. *Tim Maddocks*

The logos surrounding the central message on this plaque reflect the cooperative nature of the contemporary, privatised rail industry. *Tim Maddocks*

BRISTOL PARKWAY: Apart from the aforementioned possession in the Chipping Sodbury area, services in and out of Bristol Parkway suffered other problems on Sunday 22 August 2010. Here we see Nos 153370 and 153369 enter the station with the heavily delayed 1241 Bristol Temple Meads-Worcester Shrub Hill service, running an hour late due to a signal failure at Stapleton Road. The train would subsequently be terminated short at Cheltenham, with passengers for Ashchurch and Worcester being taken on by road.

Electrification has yet to make an appearance as an unidentified Class 221 'Super Voyager', forming 1V42, the 0610 Derby to Plymouth service, undertakes its station work in the Down platform on Wednesday 29 July 2015. Note the very large shrub growing between the then Down Goods Loop and the rear of the Down platform, which characterised parts of the station prior to the completion of the new platform and electrification works. On 10 May 2018 the Rail Minister launched a Review of Network Rail's approach to vegetation management and appointed John Varley OBE TD to chair it. The Review team was tasked with considering how Network Rail could best ensure the safety of our railways, while also protecting wildlife and preserving trees.

BRISTOL PARKWAY: The western elevation of the 2001 station building can be seen to good effect on 11 September 2010, as No 66506 waits in Stoke Gifford Down Yard with a rake of coal empty wagons for Portbury Docks.

Top left: **STOKE GIFFORD IET DEPOT:** The new depot is seen from the air on 2 April 2016. Having been built on the site of the former rail-served Filton civil engineer's tip, it is effectively complete, bar the lack of trains, which would start to arrive a few weeks later. The view is looking south-east, with Bristol Parkway station in the top left-hand corner and Filton Junction top right. The Up and Down South Wales main lines run immediately to the left of the new depot, with the Up and Down Bristol lines to the right. The freight-only line from Stoke Gifford West Junction to Filton West Junction and Hallen Marsh runs from left to right, passing under the Up and Down Bristol lines to the right of the depot.

Bottom left: **STOKE GIFFORD IET DEPOT:** The main shed and part of the yard at the new Hitachi Stoke Gifford Depot is seen on 6 June 2017, looking towards South Wales, with Hitachi-liveried sets Nos 800010 and 800005 stabled in sidings in the distance. The site is constrained by the Up and Down South Wales main lines to the north and the single freight-only line from Stoke Gifford West Junction to Filton West Junction to the south. The construction of the depot was started in the summer of 2013 by contractor Volker Fitzpatrick, with the works essentially completed by the spring of 2016. The depot effectively became operational that summer, when the first Class 800 IET train arrived at the site. The depot began to host GWR IET trains from October 2017, following their entry into passenger service on parts of the GWR network, the location being one of the key maintenance facilities for the operator's fleet.

Right: **STOKE GIFFORD IET DEPOT:** On the day of delivery and still in Hitachi livery, No 800013 moves cautiously into the main shed at the Stoke Gifford Hitachi depot on 6 June 2017, attached to another set.

Filton Abbey Wood to Barton Hill

FILTON JUNCTION: One of the more important track layout enhancements during the years before the announcement of electrification was the upgrade of the junction layout at Filton, which was upgraded from the previous single-lead junction on the South Wales route. The old arrangement, which dated from the latter years of British Rail, led to numerous delays to services in the Filton area, especially to trains running between Bristol Temple Meads and South Wales. In this scene taken on 26 March 2004, preparations are under way on the ground for the restoration of a proper double-track junction, which also involved the provision of a third platform at the nearby Filton Abbey Wood station, located just behind the cameraman.

FILTON JUNCTION: Following the completion of the junction enhancement project in June 2004, we see No 143603 working 2B68, the 0920 Bristol Temple Meads to Cardiff Central service, having just departed from Filton Abbey Wood station, which is just out of sight behind the train in this scene, looking towards Bristol Temple Meads. The unit is running over some of the new track installed as part of the scheme, which saw four tracks reinstated for a short length, before the physical junction at Filton itself was reached.

FILTON ABBEY WOOD: On 4 March 2004 No 158871, in the grey 'Alphaline' livery in use by Wessex Trains at the time, is seen working a service from Cardiff Central, as it approaches Filton Abbey Wood station. Serious work on the new third platform and enhanced junction layout has yet to begin and the original footpath from the local access road can be seen on the left. The new third platform line will be laid along its course during the forthcoming blockade.

On 28 June 2004, following the completion of the two-week blockade, No 158746 departs from the station as 1F08, the 0950 Bristol Temple Meads to Cardiff Central service, using the new track layout. The red buffer stop in the distance marked the end of a short stub of track, installed as part of the flank protection arrangements at the new junction, but being on the potential alignment of a possible fourth running line it always seemed to hint at what might be to come, something that was finally realised in November 2018 when a four-track railway was finally restored to the whole of Filton Bank. Part of the original footpath is visible to the right of the train, while the realigned station access can be seen on the left.

FILTON ABBEY WOOD: On Wednesday 6 February 2019 No 158956, in the smart new GWR dark green livery, departs from the station towards South Wales, the three-car formation reflecting the growth in passenger numbers on this busy route in recent years. The then new 'third line' of 2004 can be seen to the right of the train, as can the platform ramp of the platform built during the 2004 blockade. The train is actually running on the new fourth line, which involved the excavation of the previous embankment and a further realignment of the station access footpath. Sections of the large new DDA-compliant (Disability Discrimination Act 2005) footbridge, installed here as part of the four-tracking project in 2018, can be seen on both sides of the photograph.

By August Bank Holiday weekend in 2017, the foundations for a new retaining wall and the trackbed of the new fourth line were well under way. Note that the old pre-2004 access footpath is still visible! *Tim Maddocks/Will Salt*

FILTON ABBEY WOOD: Initial ground preparations for the new third platform line and associated works can be seen in this view taken from the footbridge, looking towards Bristol Temple Meads on 4 March 2004. The small brick wall with its decorative mural and information boards will be removed as part of the forthcoming blockade works.

By 6 February 2019 the footbridge has been reconfigured to take in the new four-platform layout at the station, as No 158956 calls forming a service to Cardiff Central. The new fourth platform is evident on the right-hand side and the girder bridge in the distance is once again spanning the four-track railway that it was originally designed to do. Keen observers of railway infrastructure will note the new signals in the 2019 view as compared with that taken in 2004, following the resignalling in connection with four-tracking and electrification and the transfer of signalling control from the 1970-vintage Bristol Panel signal box to the new Thames Valley Signalling Centre in Didcot. *MJS/Tim Maddocks*

FILTON ABBEY WOOD: Six years after the 2004 blockade, the vegetation has had a chance to recover as the driver of No 67016, on hire to FGW, enjoys a brief respite from the warmth of his driving cab as he awaits the 'right away' with the 1247 service from Paignton to Cardiff Central on 24 June 2010.

BETWEEN FILTON ABBEY WOOD AND HORFIELD: On 26 March 2004 ground preparations for the new junction points and the third running line just to the south of Filton Abbey Wood station are under way, in this view looking down the bank towards Bristol Temple Meads. The two existing running lines remained open to traffic at this time, with the adjacent worksite protected in accordance with the Rules & Regulations and risk-assessed Safe Systems of Work.

FILTON ABBEY WOOD: By 19 June 2004, during the two-week enabling blockade, the new junction points to the south of Filton Abbey Wood had been installed and plain line laid northwards towards the station. In what was the first train movement over the new line, No 66211 slowly brings support vehicles for the Kirow crane towards the worksite. The two-week blockade encompassed all lines between Patchway and Stoke Gifford East Junctions in the north and Narroways Hill Junction to the south. An amended and reduced passenger service operated via Clifton Down, Avonmouth and Henbury, with special operational arrangements being instituted at Holesmouth to facilitate the seamless movement of trains from the Severn Beach passenger line and the freight-only line on towards Henbury and Stoke Gifford.

FILTON ABBEY WOOD: The completion of a successful job! On 2 July 2004 the Mayor of Filton (whose name is sadly not recorded), Network Rail Project Manager John Hayes, Alan Wilson of Great Western Trains and David Smith of the Strategic Rail Authority celebrate the naming of vehicle No 52243 of unit No 150243 *The Filton Partnership* to mark the successful completion of the project. The four worthy and no doubt relieved gentlemen are standing on the Down Main line platform in this view looking towards Bristol Temple Meads.

FILTON ABBEY WOOD: Our four protagonists in 2004 could only have dreamed of this scene taken some 14½ years later, on 6 February 2019, as we enjoy the sight of a fully enhanced and improved four-platform station. The new and reconfigured footbridge can be seen at the north end. The station is manned for short but key periods during the peak hours, so perhaps all that is now missing is a well-appointed refreshment room? *Tim Maddocks*

FILTON ABBEY WOOD: On 11 September 2010 No 158951 leaves forming the 1230 Cardiff Central-Portsmouth Harbour service, the revised three track layout now settled in place and the inevitable vegetation firmly re-established!

BETWEEN FILTON ABBEY WOOD AND HORFIELD: In this view looking northwards on 26 March 2004, the new set of junction points has been assembled and is laid out on the formation of the former Up and Down Filton Relief lines, ready to be installed in the adjacent Up Filton Main line to the right. Virgin Trains' No 221109 passes on the Down Filton Main forming a service for Bristol Temple Meads and the South West.

HORFIELD CUTTING: From Saturday 27 October to Monday 19 November 2018, a three-week blockade took place to complete the project to reinstate the four tracks on Filton Bank. Preparatory works had been taking place along the whole of the route from Dr Days Junction to Filton Junction for several years, mostly with the two operational lines remaining open for normal traffic and some of the more complex jobs done during weekend possessions. This time the whole railway was handed over to the engineers and amended timetable arrangements put in place. Diversions via Avonmouth were not possible this time, as they had been in 2004, because the section of line from Dr Days Junction to Narroways Hill Junction was also part of the blockade, so replacement road transport was instituted with some services diverted via Box and Swindon.

In this unusual 'fisheye' view taken during that 2018 blockade, a train of auto-ballasters is standing on the new Up Filton Main line between Filton Abbey Wood and Horfield and is engaged with the construction of the new Down Filton Relief line formation. The line descends the bank towards Bristol to the right of this view. *Toby Lander*

HORFIELD CUTTING: A significant amount of preparatory work was undertaken outside of the disruptive engineering blockades, including most of the ground preparation works, a lot of civil engineering and the laying of plain track for the new running lines. On 2 April 2018 this was the view looking northwards towards the site of Horfield station. The original Up and Down Filton Main lines form the two operational running lines and the two new tracks are being laid on the formation of the **Filton Reliefs.** *Paul Walker*

ASHLEY HILL SOUTH EMBANKMENT: The sheer extent of the earthworks and associated preparations necessary just to reinstate a railway that was previously extant is apparent in this view taken near the site of the former Ashley Hill station, between Horfield and Narroways Hill Junction. This involved the construction of a 300-metre-long embankment, with widening and stabilising to retain the new Up and Down Filton Main lines. The work consisted of a 215-metre-long king-post retaining wall and about 1,500 soil nails, which ranged between 6.5 metres and 20.5 metres in length. It is a tribute to all those who planned and executed these preparatory works in the months and years leading up to the three-week blockade towards the end of 2018 that the adjacent double-track railway remained open for traffic. In this undated view taken several months before the major blockade, a 2+7 CrossCountry HST from Plymouth to Edinburgh passes the worksite at line speed.

The new works are complete in this comparative view taken shortly after the completion of the October/November 2018 blockade, and Filton Bank has a four-track railway once more. *Both Toby Lander*

NARROWAYS HILL JUNCTION: On 25 February 1995 No 6024 *King Edward I* hauls the Pathfinder Tours charter train 'The Exe-Tawe' northwards past the junction. The train had run diesel-hauled from Wolverhampton to Newton Abbot, with the steam-hauled leg starting back from Newton Abbot. No 6024 worked the train as far as Swansea, with a diesel returning the train to Wolverhampton. Following the reduction of Filton Bank from four tracks to two in 1984 with the removal of the Up and Down Filton Main lines, the two remaining running lines were slewed across from the Relief line side of the formation towards the former Main line side, in order to improve the alignment for fast running and also to provide some access for PW and S&T road vehicles. While this seemed perfectly logical for just two tracks, it did mean that a considerable amount of work would ultimately be required when the old formation was required to support four tracks again after almost 35 years. With the two operational lines in almost constant use, it was not practicable to undertake any significant slewing prior to the main 2018 blockade, but most of the new plain line was installed, ballasted and tamped prior to the start of that work, with the original two running lines remaining open. This in itself was quite an achievement and involved some temporary slewing just to get a tamper onto the newly installed sections of plain line.

Access for photography at Narroways Junction is now severely restricted, by both fencing and tree growth, but the aspect is still appealing. This image was taken from a public footpath that crosses the railway just to the north of the junction on Saturday 11 September 2010. No 143603 is taking the junction on to the single line of the Severn Beach branch as the 1203 Bristol Temple Meads to Avonmouth local service, while an unidentified HST heads for Dr Days Bridge Junction as the 1028 Swansea-Paddington service, which has been diverted due to the closure of Bristol Parkway by an engineering possession. The profusion of vegetation growth over the previous 25 years tends to mask the fact that this was formerly a four-track main line, with the line to Avonmouth having been double track, although the latter was singled when the area was resignalled in the early 1970s. Despite appearances to the contrary, this is far from being a rural area! *Ben Ashworth/MJS*

STAPLETON ROAD VIADUCT:
This is the structure that caused the four tracks of Filton Bank to be reduced to two in the 1980s, due to its deteriorating condition. In this view taken prior to its demolition over the weekend of 27 July 2017, it is clearly still capable of carrying the weight of some plant working on preparatory works for the restoration of the four tracks!

The old viaduct is seen again shortly prior to demolition, with temporary supports in place to allow phased dismantling to commence on 27th July. The temporary supports allowed the structure to be removed in small sections by tracked plant working on the ground around the base of the viaduct. Note that the A432 main road has been temporarily closed to allow the work to take place. A new steel and concrete bridge was constructed in 2018, the spans being put into place on the night of 30 June. *Both Toby Lander*

STAPLETON ROAD: Seen here in 2008, prior to the decision to reinstate the four tracks, the formation of the former Up and Down Filton Main lines between the disused platforms (on the right) was leased to the local community as a garden, known as 'Eastside Roots'. This became a successful and much-loved local amenity, but its removal was both necessary and inevitable, once the area was returned to the use for which it had originally been intended. During the early years of the four-tracking project, Network Rail worked closely with local community representatives to try to identify an alternative location for the project. The garden project was in full swing in this view taken on Saturday 4 September 2010, as local shoppers prepare to board No 143618, working the 1035 Avonmouth to Bristol Temple Meads service. The value of such small, suburban stations to their local communities in providing a convenient life-line is well illustrated here.

On 6 February 2019 former 'Thames Turbo' unit No 166207 waits to depart from the Up Filton Relief platform with a local service to Severn Beach. The contrast with the 2010 photograph could hardly be greater. The community garden is gone, of course, and the new Up and Down Filton Main lines are now fully operational. A massive and unsightly DDA-compliant footbridge, with all its attendant but legally necessary ramps, is being constructed and already completely dominates the location. Note the double-height railings on parts of the bridge, no doubt a measure to discourage vandals from throwing items onto the railway, a sad but arguably necessary indictment of the times. The new steel and concrete viaduct on the Filton Main lines over the A432 starts immediately beyond the station area in the middle distance. *MJS/Tim Maddocks*

STAPLETON ROAD VIADUCT: We take one final look at the old viaduct prior to demolition, as tracked plant removes the old decking. The Up and Down Filton Relief lines are to the left of the viaduct in this view looking northwards from the former Main line platforms.

On 5 July 2018 the new steel and concrete viaduct is in position, although work remains to be done on the parapets. Ballast and track would follow in the coming weeks. *Toby Lander/Julian Boniface*

STAPLETON ROAD: In this view looking northwards in 1981, the photographer is standing on the station footbridge above the Up and Down Filton Mains, with the old steel girder bridge in the background, just beyond the platform ramps. The four lines climb towards Narroways Hill Junction, which can just be discerned in the distance, before the main lines curve away to the right.

On 6 February 2019 No 166219 runs off the end of the new viaduct on the reopened Down Filton Main, forming a local service from Bristol Parkway to Weston-super-Mare. What appears to be a new brick platform face on the new Up Filton Main is actually nothing more than a neat finishing off of the new platform; there are currently no plans for platforms on the new Main lines at Stapleton Road or Lawrence Hill stations. *Tim Venton/Tim Maddocks*

STAPLETON ROAD: Our 1981 photographer now turns his lens southwards, as a northbound HST, possibly a cross-country working, passes through the station on the Up Filton Relief line.

Looking southwards on Sunday 30 September 2018 the plain line of the new Down Filton Main has been laid beyond the ends of the platforms and the space formerly occupied by the community garden project has been completely excavated, ready for new ballast to be laid. Note the luxurious temporary shelter on the Down platform – clearly no expense has been spared for the comfort of the citizens of **Bristol!** *Tim Venton/MJS*

LAWRENCE HILL: A collection of characterful brick buildings and cobbles are extant on the Up platform at Lawrence Hill on 22 March 1986 as single-unit 'bubble car' No B126 (W55026) departs at 1124 forming the 1120 Bristol Temple Meads to Severn Beach service. Note the full-length platforms still accessible to the potential travelling passenger and the openness and lack of vegetation. The former island platform has been truncated on the far side, where the Up and Down Filton Mains used to be, and a fence installed. While scenes such as this might evoke a degree of nostalgia among railway enthusiasts, the contemporary railway offers a far greater degree of comfort, speed and choice of services at this location. The black metal girder bridge in the background used to carry the former Midland main line from Bristol Temple Meads up to Mangotsfield, Yate and beyond, but was disused by this date and had been converted into a very useful cycle route between Bristol and Bath, using the former Midland lines throughout. *David Holmes*

LAWRENCE HILL: Turning round through 180 degrees from the 1986 photograph, and from a viewpoint on the opposite platform looking towards Dr Days Bridge Junction and Bristol Temple Meads, we see No 143618 departing as the 1035 Avonmouth to Bristol Temple Meads local service on 4 September 2010.

LAWRENCE HILL: On the same date as the previous photograph, our photographer is using the bridge carrying the A420 Church Road to good effect, as we see No 158958 arriving as the 1030 Cardiff Central-Portsmouth Harbour service. Custom on this busy route has steadily increased, despite increasingly common instances of overcrowding on the busier trains. Fortunately it proved possible to increase many sets to three cars in recent years and there are hopes that cascaded 'Thames Turbo' Class 16X sets will be deployed on this route in due course. Note the formation of the former Up and Down Filton Main lines on the right, now well and truly overgrown! The large red-brick building on the left is a supermarket, which occupies the site of the former goods yard.

A railway re-vitalised! On 6 February 2019 No 158960, still carrying the older FGW livery, passes non-stop through the station on the Down Filton Relief line with a Cardiff to Portsmouth service, while a Class 166 unit draws to a stand at the adjacent platform with a local service to Avonmouth. The mass of vegetation on the right of the platforms has now been replaced by the welcome sight of the pristine metals of the reopened Filton Main lines, now fully operational. Even the girders of the former Midland line, now carrying the busy Bristol to Bath cycle route, have been given a repaint! MJS/ Tim Maddocks

DR DAYS JUNCTION: The railway needs constant maintenance and improvement. These track works in January 2011 at Dr Days Bridge Junction, just south of Lawrence Hill, are fairly typical in that respect. On the 9th a Kirow crane is in the process of lifting heavy equipment in connection with the relaying work. This telephoto shot is looking towards Lawrence Hill station. Note the panels of new, concrete-sleepered track on the flat wagons to the right of the crane.

DR DAYS JUNCTION: Nos 66744 (Colas Rail) and 66128 (DB Schenker, but still with EWS markings) stand with their respective trains at the junction during the possession for S&C renewal on Sunday 9 October 2011. Note the dust as a remote-control 'triple whacker' flattens the trackbed for renewal of the Down Filton Relief line, while men and machines continue with other work. A workman checks his watch – it is 1039hrs!

DR DAYS JUNCTION: The actual junction can be seen in this view looking south, taken during the renewals possession on Sunday 9 October 2011. More 'men and machines' are working in the distance, close to the bridge carrying the A4320 'St Philips Causeway'. The trackbed for the Down Filton Relief line is being compacted by the 'triple whacker', prior to having new plain line laid on it. Although the majority of Filton Bank was reduced from four tracks to two in 1984, the short section of route from just south of Lawrence Hill station, through Dr Days Bridge Junction and on to Bristol East Junction has always remained as four tracks. The two lines going off to the left form what is known locally as the 'Rhubarb Loop', providing a connection to the main Box lines at North Somerset Junction.

DR DAYS JUNCTION: Newly restored by Colas Rail following a two-year 'sabbatical' at Dagenham with its previous owner, No 66847 (ex-66574) shows off a variation in Colas livery as it operates a ballast train during the same possession. The train was 'top-and-tailed' with No 66744 at the other end. Note the mechanical plant unloading ballast from the train.

BARTON HILL DEPOT: In a busy scene on 28 May 2010 No 57306 *Jeff Tracy* passes the maintenance depot, owned by DB, on the Up Filton Relief line, with 2U14, the 1102 Taunton to Cardiff service, formed from four Arriva-liveried Mark 2 coaches and with another Class 57 bringing up the rear. A four-car 'Voyager' service passes on the Down Filton Main with a service for Bristol Temple Meads. The depot seems to be full of rolling stock, ranging from bogie coal wagons and some further Mark 2 coaches. A Class 66 and an 08 diesel shunter are also 'on shed'. *Anthony Hicks*

BARTON HILL DEPOT: Prior to 2004 maintenance of Rail Express Systems (RES) locomotives and stock used on the Travelling Post Office services was undertaken here. On 14 March 1999 RES-liveried Nos 47739 *Resourceful* (later renamed *Robin of Templecombe*) and 47749 *Atlantic College* (later renamed *Demelza* and *City of Truro*) are stabled at the depot. This site used to be a wagon maintenance depot in British Rail days. An RES-liveried BG can be seen in the left background standing on one of two sidings that were formerly part of the Up and Down Midland lines from Bristol Temple Meads to Yate.

BARTON HILL DEPOT: The spire of St Mary Redcliffe church stands out in an otherwise nondescript skyline as No 60007 *Sir Nigel Gresley* **glides out of Bristol Temple Meads station and into Barton Hill Depot for servicing on 3 July 2008, prior to working the return leg of 'The Cathedrals Express' back to London Victoria.** *Phil Marsh*

Chippenham to Bath Sydney Gardens

LANGLEY CROSSING: At 6.00pm on 15 July 1979 Class 31 diesels Nos 31158 and 31153 speed westwards past the site of Langley Crossing, to the east of Chippenham. There was a signal box at this location prior to resignalling in 1966, following which the signal box closed and the gates were replaced with automatic half-barriers. These in turn were abolished and the crossing closed in 1978, in connection with operational safety requirements associated with running HST services at 125mph.
David Holmes

CHIPPENHAM EAST: The junction with the Calne branch can be seen in this view, taken from an up train on 26 August 1956. The branch was 5 miles 25 chains in length, with trains running into a bay platform at Chippenham station. Despite being well patronised, the branch closed to passenger services in September 1965, freight services having been withdrawn some two years earlier.
H. C. Casserley

CHIPPENHAM: On 11 March 1983 No 47086 powers through the station at 0900 with an Up freight service, which appears to consist of loaded stone wagons from the Mendip quarries. Note that some of the former Up sidings are still extant adjacent to the Up Main line. These had previously been part of a much greater expanse of sidings, some of which served the Westinghouse Brake & Signal Company's works just to the east of the station, on the Up side. Westinghouse had enjoyed a private siding agreement with British Railways, but this came to an end in 1976. The sidings lingered on in departmental use for a few years but were subsequently removed and the entire area to the north of the Up platform redeveloped for retail purposes, as well as a car park for rail users. *David Holmes*

CHIPPENHAM: In this view looking west towards Bristol, Nos 31120 and 31139 double-head the return leg of the 'Weymouth Wizard' service back to Swindon. These were mid-week special excursions operated by British Rail in the summer period between 1981 and 1985. The success of these services helped to secure the future of the Thingley Junction to Bradford Junction route as a passenger line, with passenger services returning and Melksham station reopening in 1985. *David Holmes*

CHIPPENHAM: On 29 October 2018 No 43185, in reproduction InterCity 'raspberry ripple' livery, arrives as an early morning Up service from Bristol Temple Meads to Paddington. The extent of the car park and retail premises on the site of the former Up sidings can be seen to the right of the train. Judging by the pattern of waiting passengers, a Down service also appears to be expected. *Paul Stanford*

CHIPPENHAM: On 10 November 1971 a train hauled by a 'Western' diesel-hydraulic arrives in the Down platform. By this date the mechanical signal boxes in Chippenham had been closed and signalling control transferred to Swindon Panel. Access to the well-filled Up sidings on the right would have been by means of ground frames released by the panel. The empty trackbed immediately to the right of the arriving train used to be a through line but was later converted into two back-to-back sidings, the western one being used as a bay platform for Weymouth trains until 1966.

On Thursday 11 July 2013 No 43153 heads 1C09, the 1000 London Paddington to Paignton service, into Platform 1. Note the absence of track in the nearside platform. This was formerly the Down platform until 1976, when it was slewed to the island platform in connection with the commencement of High Speed Train operations, requiring access to both operational platforms to be via the footbridge, although the main passenger facilities and station offices stayed on the now-disused platform, where they remain to this day. There is still no sign of the impending electrification works, but this was due to be commissioned as far as Chippenham from the Wootton Bassett direction in March 2019, thus requiring the new bi-mode IETs to operate on diesel power for the remaining 25 miles to Bristol Temple Meads. *H. C. Casserley/MJS*

THINGLEY JUNCTION SIDINGS on the Up side of the main lines were opened in January 1937 as the Central Ammunition Depot Sidings. They were built in connection with an increase in ammunition storage facilities in the area around Corsham and Box Tunnel. Some of the sidings were removed in 1966 and those that remained saw a steadily fall in usage. The site was sold by the MoD to an engineering company in 1995, but in 2001 came into use again as a long-welded-rail depot. Following the Hatfield derailment in October 2000, Railtrack and then Network Rail, needed to replace a significant amount of rail in a short space of time. Rail was imported from Europe to supplement domestic UK supplies and 60-foot lengths were welded into 360-foot lengths using a flash-butt welder, seen attached to a road-rail machine on the right of this view taken on 25 January 2001.

By 2004 the sidings were being used to store or stable certain items of rolling stock. On 23 April 2004 Loram Rail Grinder No 79257, the last of the class so far and less than a year old, is prepared for its next duty.

BETWEEN THINGLEY JUNCTION AND CORSHAM: On 20 July 1982 HST set No 253028 is seen approaching Corsham forming a Down express to Bristol Temple Meads. The introduction of Sectorisation and the InterCity 'Executive' livery was still a few years away and the set looks smart in the original blue and grey livery applied to HSTs when they were first introduced. Note the two signal heads on the gantry towards the rear of the train. That situated at the end of the gantry applied to movements over the Up Main line in the wrong (Down) direction. *John Acton, MJS collection*

CORSHAM: On 9 May 1953 No 4969 *Shugborough Hall* arrives at Corsham with an Up train. Although there are passengers waiting on the Up platform, the first vehicle behind the tender indicates that this may be a parcels or departmental working. No 4969 entered traffic in December 1929 and was withdrawn in September 1962. Corsham station was located in a cutting, with the main station buildings up at road level and more rudimentary facilities down on the platforms. Siding space in and around the station was limited, although what space was available was utilised to the full, with a small number of sidings provided for local stone traffic. The station was closed on 4 January 1965, when the local service between Bath Spa and Chippenham was withdrawn. *Colour-Rail collection*

CORSHAM: The cramped nature of the location is further evident in this view of No 5084 *Reading Abbey* passing Corsham signal box with a Down express in 1959. Note the immaculate rake of Mark 1 coaches in chocolate and cream livery. The roof of the goods shed can be seen above the third coach and the Down sidings still appear busy. The Up platform of the passenger station can just be discerned beyond the rear coach of the train.

From a similar vantage point on 29 July 2015, during the major Box Tunnel and Bathampton blockade, we can see that the former goods shed is still extant, although all sidings and pointwork are now long gone. Stone from local quarries continued to be loaded into trains at Corsham until around 1960, and goods facilities were withdrawn from here in 1963. *A. Sainty collection/MJS*

CORSHAM: From a vantage point on the Down side of the line slightly to the east of the signal box, we see No 5000 *Launceston Castle* approaching the station in 1956 with an Up stopping service. Although express locomotives fresh out of overhaul at Swindon Works were used on local trains on 'running-in' turns, this particular engine seems a little too grubby, unless it required rather more running-in than usual!

The same bridge confirms that this is a photograph of the same location, taken on Wednesday 29 July 2015 during the six-week blockade of Box Tunnel and Bathampton Junction. A group of engineering staff await the arrival of the 'Man Rider' to take them from the nearby access point, where they will have signed in to the worksite, to the mouth of Box Tunnel. *P. Alexander/MJS*

BOX TUNNEL: During the six-week blockade in the summer of 2015, Network Rail undertook major track renewal works at Bathampton Junction and in Box Tunnel. In the latter, each running line was removed in turn and the formation excavated by contractors Babcock to a lower level, to facilitate the necessary clearances for the 25kV overhead wires that were planned to follow later. This meant that both Up and Down Main lines through the tunnel and on its approaches were completely renewed with new track, a total of some 6 miles of plain line. At the time this was the biggest track renewal possession ever in terms of length of blockade and the amount of work completed. It required a very significant logistics support programme, which included the operation of a total of 217 engineering trains to service the various renewal worksites within the blockade. One of these trains, 6W32, is seen here standing on the Up Main line at the east end of Box Tunnel, being loaded with spent ballast to be taken to Westbury.

BOX TUNNEL: In a slightly wider-angled view of 6W32 on the same date, No 66200 waits for the completion of loading of spent ballast before leaving the site. Box Tunnel can be seen in the background.

BOX TUNNEL: In what is believed to be a photograph taken during the Edwardian era, we see the London-end portal of the tunnel on what appears to be a very cold winter's day, judging by the amount of ice on the walls of the cutting. The presence of the signal wire in the '6 foot' indicates that Box Tunnel East signal box was still open. This closed in 1910, together with the connection just behind the camera from the Up Main to the siding that led into the underground stone quarries on the right. From that date, rail access to the underground loading platform approximately 200 yards beyond the small tunnel portal, serving the very extensive Corsham Down and adjacent Box Hill quarries, was from a connection established nearer Corsham station in 1876 via the siding in this view. Note that the siding still has the old 'baulk road'. A wagon loaded with dressed Bath stone stands just outside the low-roofed quarry tunnel entrance. At the time these wagons would have been worked by horses up to the goods yard at Corsham.

We fast-forward over 100 years now to 29 July 2015. The arch of the tunnel portal has been strengthened with engineer's blue bricks in the interim and it is just possible to discern how the tunnel roof reduces to normal loading gauge just a few yards inside. At this stage of the six-week blockade, the Down Main line was being relaid with new concrete-sleepered track. The headlights of a loco at the head of an engineer's train a few hundred yards inside the tunnel can be seen, as can the commencement of the 1 in 100 gradient down towards Box. The portal of the tunnel into the stone quarries is still extant behind the vegetation. Quarrying ceased around 1930, but from 1938 the Government established a huge ammunition storage depot in the old stone quarries, which remained in use until 1962. The rail connection was finally removed in 1974. *MJS collection/MJS*

BOX TUNNEL: Just inside the eastern portal the lower alignment of the new track is clearly visible when compared to the adjacent Up line, which has yet to be relaid. The new rail for the Down line can be seen laid in the '4 foot' of the Up line.

BOX TUNNEL: about halfway through the 3,212-yard-long tunnel, some of the party, including one of your authors, pose for the camera and a rest during the long walk! Note that the relaying of the Down line hadn't reached this location as yet.

BOX TUNNEL: Inside the tunnel on 22 July 2015, looking west, we see a group of contractor's staff discussing the work at hand. The 'head of ballast' on the excavated Down line formation can be seen just ahead of the piece of tracked plant. The considerable depth to which the renewed Down Main formation has been excavated is clear when compared to the still-extant Up Main line. *Tim Maddocks*

BOX TUNNEL: Further along the tunnel the new bottom ballast is being compacted using a remote-controlled 'double whacker'. Note the face masks, which are now mandatory in such dusty environments.

BOX TUNNEL: During one of our inspection visits, on Wednesday 22 July 2015, your authors were part of a larger group that was accompanied by a COSS ('Controller of Site Safety'). Such individuals form part of the larger framework of staff involved in managing the health and safety of all staff and activities within large, complex Network Rail worksites, and each COSS signs in with an overarching 'Engineering Supervisor' ('ES') each time they take a group into the possession. The 'ES' often has an overview of a larger area of the possession. On this occasion, a problem with the drainage works developed during our walk and necessitated a prolonged stop in the middle of the tunnel so that solutions could be identified and implemented. It became necessary for our 'COSS' to leave the group and do something more urgent elsewhere, leaving our group in the care of a 'static' COSS and thus with no estimate as to when we could resume our walk through the tunnel and eventually return to daylight! Fortunately another 'COSS' turned up, who was able to accompany us onwards to the tunnel exit.

BOX TUNNEL: Deep inside the tunnel taken a week later on 29 July 2015, a TXM Plant road-rail machine operates alongside the newly laid Down Main line. The concrete sleepers are sitting on the new bottom ballast and are now awaiting top ballast and tamping.

BOX TUNNEL: On an unrecorded date prior to the nationalisation of the railways in 1948, 'Saint' Class 4-6-0 No 2939 *Croome Court* emerges from the magnificent western portal of Box Tunnel with a Down express. The open wagons are stabled in the headshunt for Pictor's stone siding, which was accessed via the trailing connection in the Up Main visible in the photo. Pictor & Sons was one of several stone companies in the area; they combined in 1887 to form the Bath Stone Firms Ltd, which by 1911 had become the Bath & Portland Stone Firms Ltd.

On 22 July 2015, during the first week of the six-week blockade, the facade of the western portal remains as impressive as ever, as a rake of JNAs forms part of the consist of engineer's train 6W43. Work is under way to relay the Down Main line on the lower alignment to accommodate the future installation of overhead electric wires, the lower level being clearly apparent in this photo. *R. M. Casserley collection/MJS*

BOX TUNNEL: The lineside is neat and tidy and the ballast shoulder immaculate in this 1956 view of No 7019 *Fowey Castle* leaving the tunnel and passing Box's Down distant signal with an express train composed of 'blood and custard' Mark I coaches. The connection into Pictor's siding is still extant, although the headshunt seen in the previous picture appears to have been removed. The siding would eventually be lifted in 1959 as stone quarrying in the area contracted.

On 22 July 2015 our viewpoint is slightly further to the west and shows the attractive stone overbridge carrying the A4 road. Engineer's staff congregate around the tunnel portal, where the relaying site of the Down Main line started. Note the significant increase in lineside vegetation as compared with the orderliness of the 1956 view. *Colour-Rail, MJS collection/MJS*

BOX MILL LANE HALT: Looking east from the end of the Up platform on 25 September 1960, we see Nos 6972 *Beningbrough Hall*, 6830 *Buckenhill Grange* and 6981 *Marbury Hall* heading west. The three arches of the A4 road overbridge near the west end of Box Tunnel can be seen in the background.

The rather basic facilities provided at the halt can be seen in the second view taken on the same day. The Halt, at milepost 101¼, was opened by the GWR in 1930 and was closer to and more convenient for the centre of the village than the main Box station. The halt was closed, together with most of the other local stations between Bath and Chippenham, on 4 January 1965.
Both H. C. Casserley

BOX MILL LANE: On 17 September 1975 No 50011 *Centurion* is about to pass the site of Box Mill Lane Halt with an Up express formed of Mark 2 coaches and a Mark 1 buffet typical of the immediate pre-HST period. The 198-yard-long Middle Hill Tunnel is in the background. *Tom Heavyside*

Further reading...

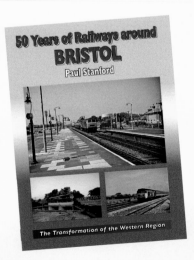

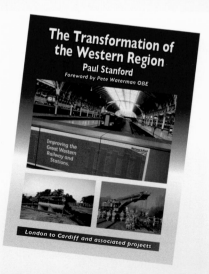

If you are enjoying this look back at the past and present journey from Swindon to Bristol then you might like to read more on the transformation of the Western Region of Britain's rail network.

These two volumes may be of interest.

ISBN 978 1 85794 566 9 Due Spring 2020

ISBN: 978 1 85794 544 7

MIDDLE HILL TUNNEL: A standard-gauge Down train emerges from the west end of Middle Hill Tunnel in 1883. Both lines appear to be mixed gauge, as the broad gauge would not be finally abolished until 1892.

The tunnel appears as impressive as ever in the second view taken on 14 April 1980, as HST set No 253013 emerges forming the 1320 Paddington to Bristol Temple Meads service. The Bath stone facade has been repaired with bricks at some point since the 1883 photograph.

The elegant facade is seen to good advantage in the third view looking east on 22 July 2015 during the six-week blockade. The Down Main line has already been relaid but not yet tamped. *R. M. Casserley collection/Brian Morrison/MJS*

BOX: This undated view looking eastwards was possibly taken during the Edwardian period and shows the complete station and railway environs. The wharf for loading Bath stone can be seen, together with the loading cranes and a few wagons awaiting loading. The locomotive shed appears to be in use; it was provided to house banking engines for Up goods services through Box Tunnel and beyond as far as **Wootton Bassett**. *MJS collection*

BOX: The former loco shed is seen on 5 July 1936. It closed in 1919, after more powerful locomotives were provided for goods services. Following the closure the shed was used by the Engineers Department. A water tank on a masonry base has been built on the site of the siding leading into the shed. *R. M. Casserley collection*

BOX station still appears substantially complete in this view dated 25 September 1960, although the former Bath stone wharf seems to be disused and is becoming overgrown. Goods facilities were withdrawn in 1963 and Box station itself closed on 4 January 1965.

The modern-day angle on 22 July 2015 approximates to the site of the former platforms. Middle Hill Tunnel is a common feature and the area adjacent to the running lines is full of containers and other equipment associated with the ongoing blockade. *R. M. Casserley/MJS*

BOX: Turning our camera through 180 degrees, we now look west on the same date as the previous photograph. The station approach road is now hidden by vegetation to the left of the railway, whereas the sites of the former stone wharf and old loco shed appear to have been sold, due to the presence of a more modern boundary fence, itself largely hidden from view by the inevitable vegetation.

BOX: That vegetation is not a recent phenomenon, as evidenced by this view taken from above Middle Hill Tunnel looking west on 20 July 1982, as an Up HST passes the site of Box station and goods yard.
John Acton, MJS collection

BATHAMPTON: This is the view from the minor road overbridge just to the west of the junction on 22 July 2015, day 5 of the 45-day blockade. For the first two weeks the possession of the main lines started just east of Bathampton Junction and ran as far as Thingley Junction (exclusive), meaning that normal passenger services could still run from Bristol Temple Meads via Bath Spa and Trowbridge and vice versa. In this view, Colas Rail Matisa B41UE tamper No 75407 stands over the physical junction, on the open railway, awaiting permission to enter the blockade on the 'wrong line'. The Trowbridge line curves away to the right. The possession protection and attendant hand signalman can just be discerned in the distance. The general area in the foreground is the site of the former Bathampton Junction station, which closed in October 1966.

Two weeks later, on 5 August 2015, the blockade limits have been extended to form a 'Y' shape, running from Bath Spa to Thingley Junction and Bradford Junction (all exclusive). Passenger services then terminated at Bath Spa and were replaced by buses onwards to Chippenham and Westbury. This allowed major relaying worksites to commence at Bathampton Junction itself (S&C renewals), Dundas Aqueduct on the Trowbridge line (lowering of track to permit W8 gauge for container trains) and other plain line renewal locations between Bathampton and Bath Spa. Here we see some drainage works being undertaken at Bathampton, prior to the start of the junction S&C renewal a short while later. Framed by the road-rail machine's jib, No 66847 waits with 6C36, the 1542 (Tuesday) Bescot to Bath Spa spoil train. The train was 'top and tailed', with No 60056 on the other end.

BATHAMPTON: We move forward another week to 12 August 2015 and the relaying of the junction has started. No 60096 stands on the Up Main line at the head of 6X38, with wagons conveying track panels, while on the right Freightliner No 66519 is passing cautiously on the Down Main with 6T40, conveying ballast side-tippers and sleepers, about to swing round onto the Up Trowbridge line. The Down Trowbridge line has been removed and the formation dug out. A new under-track membrane can be seen just around the curve in the distance.

A week later, on 19 August, we see the renewal of the junction trackwork almost completed, with just the tamping to be finished. A recent rainstorm highlights the new fittings, as a road-railer and another engineer's train stand on the Down Trowbridge line. The red marker boards on the track read 'STOP. Check points are set correctly before proceeding'; this underlines the fact that during many possessions the normal signalling is disconnected and great care must be observed by all concerned to ensure that rail movements are made safely.

BATHAMPTON: On 19 September 1936 Southern Railway 'U' Class 'Mogul' No 1624 passes Bathampton station with the 2.04pm Portsmouth to Bristol service. The signal box is out of view behind the train at the London end of the Down platform; it would be replaced in 1956 by a new, brick-built box, which stood adjacent to the Up Main line, just off the London end of the Up platform. This in turn would close in 1970, when multiple aspect signalling was introduced, controlled from Bristol Panel. *H. C. Casserley*

BATHAMPTON: With the honey-coloured terraces of Bath climbing the distant hillside, No 31135 passes Bathampton on Tuesday 19 July 1983 with the Malago Vale to Old Oak Common empty vans, recalling a time when traffic such as newspapers, mail and Red Star Parcels was conveyed by rail. The signal head above the first vehicle is the signal controlling the exit from the Up Goods Loop.

During the first week of the Bathampton and Box blockade on 22 July 2015 No 153325 hurries west at Bathampton as 2M97, the 0823 Southampton Central to Great Malvern stopper. No 75407, a Colas Rail Matisa B41UE tamper, travels in the opposite direction as the 0935 Bristol Kingsland Road S&T to Bathampton Junction engineer's movement, prior to entering the blockade a short while later. *John Acton, MJS collection/MJS*

BATHAMPTON: Moving forward to Wednesday 5 August 2015, 6C36, the 1542 (Tuesday) Bescot to Bath Spa spoil train, stands on the Down Main at Bathampton, as a road-rail machine unloads pipes for the ongoing drainage works at the junction, behind the photographer. The train was 'top and tailed', with No 60056 in view at the Bath end.

Two weeks later a recent rainstorm highlights part of the almost completed renewals site on 19 August. Two tampers are at work fettling the new track.

BETWEEN BATHAMPTON AND SYDNEY GARDENS: On 22 May 2013 power car No 43159 leads a Down Paddington to Bristol Temple Meads train as it passes the entrance to the adjacent Up Goods Loop. The minor road bridge from which several of the previous photographs were taken can just be discerned in the distance behind the train. *Anthony Hicks*

HAMPTON ROW: Just east of Sydney Gardens, Bath, on Wednesday 12 August 2015 No 70807 heads 6T41, a consist of side-tippers filled with ballast. The train had run from Westbury via Taunton (reverse) and Bristol Temple Meads and would return empty to Westbury, after having unloaded its ballast in the blockade.

SYDNEY GARDENS, BATH: Situated a short way to the north-east of the city centre, Sydney Gardens have been a tranquil location for Bathonians to take their ease for more than 200 years. Laid out towards the end of the 18th century, the pleasure gardens would see the arrival of the Great Western Railway less than 50 years later. In this image, taken prior to the removal of the broad gauge in 1892, standard-gauge 'Queen' Class 2-2-2 No 1120 passes with a Down stopping train composed of six-wheeled vehicles. The elegant stone retaining wall behind the train supports the Kennet & Avon Canal above. Note the classic mixed-gauge 'baulk road'.

Another classic Western loco is seen approximately 90 years later, on an unrecorded date in 1976, as No D1036 *Western Emperor* passes with a Down express. *G.W. Shott/MJS collection*

SYDNEY GARDENS, BATH: In a scene familiar to one of your authors when he was living in the city, No 33001 passes at precisely 1728 on 10 August 1980 with the 1515 Portsmouth to Bristol Temple Meads service, composed of the usual five Mark 1 coaches.

Thirty-five years later No 158957 is running in the opposite direction, from Cardiff to Portsmouth, on 22 July 2015. Sadly, the carefree days of being able to sit innocently on the low balustrade wall are now long gone, due to a small minority trespassing on the railway at this location over the years and spoiling it for the majority. Railtrack and (from 2002) Network Rail had long wanted to erect a more substantial fence in conjunction with the stone parapet, in order to remove the trespass risk. Despite protracted negotiations with local planners and offers to fund various designs of elaborate, tasteful iron railings, agreement could not be reached, so everyone has instead been left with this ugly and surely ineffectual compromise of a wooden 'stockade' fence, which has been spoiling this otherwise elegant location for many years. *David Holmes/Tim Maddocks*

Bath Spa to Bristol Temple Meads

BATH SPA: For part of the six-week blockade in 2015, Bath Spa temporarily acted as a terminus station, due to the line ahead being renewed in various locations. No 43018 stands in the pouring rain at what was now the rear of 1Z10, the 1128 Bath Spa to Paignton service, which will run 'wrong line' from Platform 2 to the crossovers at Bath Goods.

BATH SPA: For a few years the Class 180s could occasionally be seen operating through Bath Spa on Bristol Temple Meads to London services. On 30 August 2003 No 180109 departs as an Up service.

The scene was dramatically transformed during the April 2017 blockade, when Network Rail undertook work to widen the platforms at Bath Spa and relay the track to facilitate the planned electrification project. On 9 April No 70801 heads east through the station with a load of track panels. At this stage the Down line was being relaid but the Up line remained open for both Up and Down services, the latter using the reversible signalling facility between the crossovers at Bathampton and Bath Goods.

BATH SPA: Seen from the London end of the Up platform on an unknown date in the 1960s, No D855 *Triumph* approaches the station with a Down express. Note the semaphore signalling (which dates the photograph to before 1968) and the complexity of the pointwork. The diverging routes from the tandem turnout in the foreground led to the Up Bay platform (left) and the two middle sidings (right). The bay platform was originally used for the Bath to Swindon stopping services, which ceased in January 1965.

From an almost identical angle on 22 May 2013 No 66194 passes with 6W97, a Hinksey to Wildmill engineer's train. The semaphores and pointwork are long gone but at least the backdrop of elegant Bath stone houses on Bathwick Hill remains. *MJS collection/Anthony Hicks*

BATH SPA: This classic view shows the station during the period between the introduction of MAS here in 1968 and the widening of the platforms in 2017. On 17 September 1975 No 31165 is seen with an Up parcels working. Note the base of the old elevated signal box in the Downside platform canopy. The wide space between the platforms was formerly occupied by two sidings, which were used to stable rolling stock between workings. The site of the old Up Bay platform can be seen to the right of the locomotive, although there was no longer any track in it by this date.

During the April 2017 blockade, when the Down line was being relaid and the Down platform widened, we see No 70801 once again, heading east through Platform 2 on the Up Reversible line with an engineering train on 9 April. *Tom Heavyside/MJS*

BATH SPA: We take a closer look at the engineering work site on 9 April. The Down line has been removed and work to widen the platform is ongoing. The basis for the widening was the innovative use of robust polystyrene blocks, some of which can be seen stacked on the platform.

BATH SPA: On the same date as the previous photographs, we see the worksite from the opposite end of the platform. Note the footings going in for the new brick face of the rebuilt platform. Pre-cast concrete platform coping stones are stockpiled on the left. The new long welded rails for the Down line have been laid out ready in the '4 foot' of the Up Main, together with rails for the relaying of the latter line.

A few days later, on 15 April 2017, the works are almost complete. The additional width of the platform is hardly noticeable, but closer examination will show that the edge of the platform canopy no longer matches the platform edge. The new clearances are, however, ready for the overhead electric wires, whenever a decision is made to complete this section of route.

BATH SPA: On 15 April 2017 the blockade included both lines through Bath Spa. In this view we can see work starting on relaying the Up platform line, as a road-rail machine moves a length of long welded rail out from the '4 foot' of the old track.

BATH SPA: On Sunday 9 April 2017 pre-formed concrete coping stones for the new platform edge are being delivered by a road-railer. The tower of St Mark's church, now a community centre, can be seen behind the top of the Up platform canopy.

BATH SPA: On 12 August 1999 No 37422 *Robert F. Fairlie*, still in Regional Railways colours, arrives with the 1303 Bristol Temple Meads to Weymouth service. Few would believe today that the area behind the locomotive used to be a small goods depot, with its own platform angled back away from the current alignment of the Up line. Goods wagons were moved around a number of stub sidings and wagon turntables by a shunting horse, which had its own small brick-built stable next to the Up line, approximately behind the first coach of the train. The goods depot, which supplemented the much larger goods facility at Westmoreland Road, to the west of the station, was finally closed and removed in 1960. This then enabled the Up platform to be lengthened.

The Up platform was further extended during the 2017 blockade, to permit full-length electric trains to be platformed. On Sunday 28 May 2017 No 43189 arrives at the newly extended platform as 1A22, the 1455 Bristol Temple Meads to London Paddington service.

BATH SPA: Viewed from Rossiter Road on the south side of the River Avon on 17 September 1975, the prototype HST arrives forming the 1348 Weston-super-Mare to Paddington service. What appears to be a walkway along the right-hand abutment of the river bridge was, in fact, a short narrow-gauge tramway, which served the former electricity works on the north bank of the Avon, close to the station, the site of which is now the new Bath bus station. *Tom Heavyside*

BATH SPA: The A367 Wells Road curves round to pass under the railway via an underbridge out of shot on the left, as No 33005 powers away from the station with a Portsmouth to Bristol working on 5 October 1980. *Tom Heavyside*

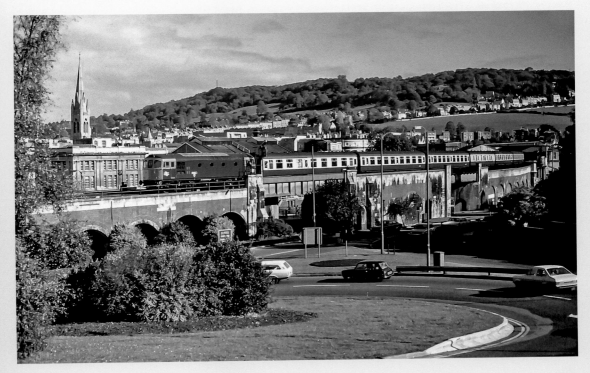

BATH GOODS: Situated approximately half a mile to the west of Bath Spa station, 'Bath Goods' is the name now given to the two main-to-main crossovers that facilitate reversible working between here and Bristol East Depot or Bathampton. However, in the past this was the site of two goods yards. 'Westmoreland Road' is a set of sidings on the Down side of the line and was until recently the location of the former waste transfer station, where refuse from Bath was transferred to rail-mounted containers for disposal at a landfill site in Buckinghamshire. 'Bath Goods' proper was the main GWR goods yard for the Bath area, located on the Up side of the line. The bulk of the former goods shed can be seen on the left of this photo, now in private use. During the second major blockade in April 2016, both Up and Down lines and all the S&C was relaid at this location. Here on 9 April, looking east towards Bath Spa station, we can see that the Down line has already been relaid and work is ongoing to renew the Up line. The new points in the immediate foreground control the entrance to the Up Goods Loop.

In pouring rain on the same day, No 70807 arrives on site with engineer's train 6C24, a consist of side-tipplers, to unload bottom ballast onto the membrane on the Up Main formation. The spire of St Matthew's church, Widcombe, can be seen above the rear of the train.

OLDFIELD PARK: 'Sprinter' No 150278 approaches with the 1528 First Great Western service from Warminster to Great Malvern on 22 June 2010. During its journey this service is booked to call at four stations that were listed for closure in the Beeching Report; of these Freshford and Avoncliff Halt never closed, while Yate and Coaley for Dursley have both subsequently reopened. Oldfield Park itself was opened in February 1929, in response to the growth of housing in that part of the city. The exit of the Up Goods Loop can be seen behind the train. The site of the 2016 relaying photographs at Bath Goods is just beyond the girder overbridge in the distance. *Phil Horton*

TWERTON TUNNEL: The castellated western portal of the longer of the two Twerton Tunnels (264 yards) is pleasantly framed by the surrounding landscape as No 31419 passes with a Portsmouth to Cardiff train on 25 October 1980. The train will run via Bristol Temple Meads, where the locomotive will either run round its train or be replaced by another loco.

On the same day HST set No 253012 passes forming a Paddington to Bristol working. Almost immediately behind the leading power car is the site of Twerton Tunnel signal box, which controlled access to the former Down Refuge siding, located to the right of the passing HST. The siding was taken out of use in 1950 and the signal box closed ten years later.

Both Tom Heavyside

TWERTON TUNNEL: The western suburbs of Bath feature in the background as ex-Southern Railway 'U' Class 2-6-0 passes on 13 September 1997 with a charter train, heading towards Bristol Temple Meads. This is the only 'U' Class locomotive to have run in preservation and is currently located on the Swanage Railway, awaiting overhaul. *Ben Ashworth*

SALTFORD: On the 1½-mile embankment between Saltford and Newton Meadows, to the west of Bath, No 6806 *Blackwell Grange* has shut off steam as it approaches Saltford station with a Swindon to Bristol stopping service on 19 September 1960. The locomotive looks to be in a very clean condition, so this is possibly a running-in turn, after having been outshopped from Swindon Works. Saltford station was located just to the west of this location and was one of four local stations between Bath Spa and Bristol Temple Meads listed for closure by the Beeching Report. Fortunately, two of the four (Oldfield Park and Keynsham) survived, but Saltford and St Anne's Park closed in 1970. The very significant road congestion on the parallel A4 road means that there is now much support locally for the possible reopening of the station, but so far nothing has materialised. *Ben Ashworth*

KEYNSHAM: On Monday 4 April 2016, during the second blockade, a TXM Plant Ltd-owned Philmor tracked digger is at work during the nine-day possession lowering the track under the road bridge (in the distance) and renewing the station platforms in preparation for the forthcoming electrification. In this view looking west towards Bristol, the Down line has already been relaid.

The girder bridge carries a local road over the station, and is one of the key structures in the area that required the track level to be lowered, to facilitate clearances for the overhead electric wires. Work continues on the Up line formation on the same day.

KEYNSHAM: It would have been rather embarrassing if the engineers had failed to leave sufficient room for the new Down line, but fortunately the measurements were correct! The new rail for the Down line is laid out ready in the '4 foot' of the Up Main in this view from Keynsham station looking towards Bristol. The line crosses Keynsham Hams on an embankment just beyond the two signals, the southern side of which used to be emblazoned with the name 'Somerdale', reflecting the original name of the station, 'Keynsham & Somerdale'. Although neglected and overgrown in more recent times, the name can still just be made out in a 'Google Satellite' image. The Somerdale area of the town was well known for the rail-served Fry's chocolate factory. It was more recently owned by Cadbury, which proposed its closure in 2007. A local campaign to save the site was ultimately unsuccessful when Cadbury was sold to Kraft Foods in 2010 and, a year later, the Keynsham chocolate factory was closed. The regeneration plans for the site involve the inevitable new housing, a retirement 'village', shops and a school.

On 4 April 2016 No 66528 *Madge Eliot MBE* creeps into the engineering worksite with 6T30, the 0821 rake of JNAs and sand wagons from Hinksey (via Badminton and Filton), ultimately bound for Westbury.

ST ANNE'S PARK: This is the site of the station around 1890, with the 154-yard Bristol No 2 Tunnel in the background. The station opened in 1898 as the suburbs around Bristol grew in size and population.

The station closed, together with Saltford, in 1970, but the site of the former Down platform can be discerned next to the carriages of the train in this view taken on 23 April 1983 with No 33026 working a Portsmouth to Bristol service. The headshunt adjacent to the Up Main line served the large marshalling yard of Bristol East Depot, located a short way further towards Bristol, but the yards had closed to general goods traffic in 1967, being retained for engineer's use and the storage of redundant vehicles for some years thereafter. *R. M. Casserley collection/Tom Heavyside*

BRISTOL EAST DEPOT: On 8 September 1987 an Up HST passes as the 1410 Bristol Temple Meads to Paddington service. The former Up yard is now almost empty and would, in due course, be lifted and redeveloped. At one time there was even a 'hump' to aid marshalling. The Down yard was being used by the Civil Engineer at the time and is full of ballast hoppers and other engineering wagons. It survives today, albeit in an extremely simplified and reduced form. It was used for steel traffic by EWS (later DB Schenker) in the early 2000s, and more recently has also been used as a compound in connection with ongoing renewal works in the Bristol area. *Tom Heavyside*

ST PHILIPS MARSH: Churchward 2-8-0 No 2818 is seen on shed on 29 April 1950. Built in 1905, the loco retained inside steam pipes to the end and was withdrawn in October 1963 and went straight into preservation as part of the National Collection. In 2018 the locomotive was moved to STEAM Museum of the Great Western Railway at Swindon. Located next to the Bristol Temple Meads Avoiding Line, St Philips Marsh shed was opened in 1910 and was mainly a depot for goods engines. It was closed in 1964.

Although the site of the former steam depot was redeveloped for non-railway use, an HST depot of the same name opened nearby in 1975. On 14 March 1999 No 43182 forms part of a set stabled in the depot sidings, wearing the smart Great Western Trains livery of the time. *H. C. Casserley/MJS*

ST PHILIPS MARSH: Seen in the depot on 2 September 2010 are 'Sprinters' Nos 150234 and 143621 receiving fitters' attention. SPM shares most of the maintenance work on the GWR DMU fleet with the larger DMU depot at Exeter, although it is the latter location that is the primary site for this work.

BRISTOL TEMPLE MEADS: The east end of the station is seen from the cab of an approaching train on 28 July 2001. The ugly grey bulk of the former Post Office conveyor bridge stands out prominently at the London end of the platforms. Thankfully this was removed at Christmas 2015, having become an eyesore since Royal Mail stopped using it in 2000. The old Royal Mail building adjacent to the east side of Temple Meads is now to be refurbished as a campus, thus further regenerating this part of the city.
Phil Marsh

BRISTOL TEMPLE MEADS: Running 15 minutes early when photographed on Wednesday 21 September 2016, No 66571 stands on the Up Through line at Bristol Temple Meads and waits for a proceed aspect with the 1625 Bristol West Depot to Southampton MCT. To the right, No 43147 will soon head 1A25, the 1630 Bristol Temple Meads to London Paddington service. The signals in the picture are still controlled by Bristol Panel, but this would change from 2018, when the £130 million third stage of a four-stage £250 million resignalling programme would start, covering the Bristol Temple Meads area. The lines through Bristol Parkway had already been resignalled and control transferred to the Thames Valley Signalling Centre at Didcot. The fourth and final stage through Bath was scheduled to be completed during Easter 2019. This will then leave just the section of line between Bristol West and Bridgwater controlled by the remnants of the 1970 Bristol Panel signal box. Network Rail currently has no firm plans to resignal this section of line, as it was not part of the original electrification proposals.

BRISTOL TEMPLE MEADS GOODS DEPOT: The former goods depot adjacent to Temple Meads was at one time the largest covered area in Britain, covering some 5 acres. It was opened in 1924 to replace and expand an older facility. Following the decline in goods traffic on British Railways, the depot was latterly used for parcels traffic, but was finally closed and demolished in 1982. In this view, dating from 1978, parcels vans are standing on what were known as the 'High Level Sidings', but which used to form part of a through goods-only route to Bristol Docks and ultimately Ashton Junction, on the Portishead branch. The lower-level sidings are also still in use and the slim wooden Bristol Goods signal box is still extant. The boundary of the Bristol Panel compound is demarcated by a low wire mesh fence.

At the site of the depot on 4 May 2019, the track of Platform 1, the panel outbuildings and the distant spire of St Mary Redcliffe are our common denominators with the 'past' view, but everything else has changed beyond recognition. The site of the former covered goods depot lay derelict for many years, but modern office blocks, some with ground-floor retail premises, were eventually built in the early 2000s, one suite of which was even temporarily used as the local Network Rail Area HQ for a few months in 2003. The inevitable palisade security fence has replaced the more casual wire mesh and an equally inevitable buddleia bush lurks within. Just one of the former sidings beyond Platform 1 remains in use, known as the 'High Level Siding', but even that doesn't go far beyond the palisade fence. The remainder of the former High Level Sidings area is now used for car parking and a pedestrian access route to the new offices and retail premises. *Tim Venton/Tim Maddocks*

BRISTOL TEMPLE MEADS: Back in the 'good old days', former GWR diesel railcars Nos W36 and W35, with an ordinary coach marshalled between, stand in the old Platform 2 (now Platform 13) on 23 April 1954 forming a local service. Note the scissors crossovers, to permit flexible use of the long platform face. *David Holmes*

BRISTOL TEMPLE MEADS: This delightful view of pannier tank No 3746 on station pilot duties at the west end of the station was taken on 2 August 1958. The loco and wagon are standing on what is now the Up Middle Siding. *David Holmes*

BRISTOL TEMPLE MEADS: On 1 July 1961 No 4096 *Highclere Castle* stands at Platform 9 with the 11.45am Bristol Temple Meads to Paddington express. Note the large water tower beyond the platform canopy. *David Holmes*

BRISTOL TEMPLE MEADS: The 1930s colour light signalling is apparent in this view, taken on 26 August 1956 looking towards the south-west through the 1874 Digby Wyatt train shed. No 5094 *Tretower Castle* approaches on the Up Through line, while 2-6-0 No 6391 waits with its train in Platform 9.

The modern-day view is undoubtedly cleaner, brighter and thus more inviting for the travelling public, but possibly less interesting for the railway enthusiast. On the dull early spring morning of 29 March 2011 CrossCountry 'Voyager' set No 221132 waits in what is now Platform 3 forming the 1006 Paignton to Manchester Piccadilly service. To the left, 'Sprinter' No 143612 is about to depart from Platform 5 with a local service to Severn Beach. *R. M. Casserley/MJS*

BRISTOL TEMPLE MEADS: On 3 September 2010 No 143620 waits at Platform 5 for any last-minute custom while forming the 1116 service to Severn Beach.

BRISTOL TEMPLE MEADS: On 8 September 1987 power car No 43002 heads the 1035 service to Paddington, formed with a set in the then new 'InterCity Executive' livery. The Post Office conveyor bridge, then very much in use, dominates the scene. *Tom Heavyside*

BRISTOL TEMPLE MEADS: The cream and brown glazed bricks of the 1934 platform buildings are seen to good effect in this view taken on Platform 7 on 28 June 2004. By the late Edwardian period Bristol Temple Meads was becoming increasingly congested and plans were drawn up by the GWR in 1914 to extend and resignal the station, but these were not implemented due to the First World War. No further work was done during the 1920s, during which time traffic levels at busy times resulted in significant congestion and huge delays. Finally in 1929 the GWR was able to take advantage of a Government scheme to promote large capital projects. Work to rebuild the station and provide new platforms and also to resignal the area was started in 1930 and completed in 1935.

BRISTOL TEMPLE MEADS: Our earlier mention of the Bristol to Bath cycle route, which runs along the former Midland line, reflects the enormous increase in the popularity of cycling in the Bristol area in recent years, as evidenced here by the massive provision for cycles at Bristol Temple Meads. The former bay Platform 2 and Motorail Dock can be glimpsed in the background of this view taken on 4 May 2019, looking west along Platforms 3 and 4. *Tim Maddocks*

BRISTOL TEMPLE MEADS: On the morning of Wednesday 12 August 2015, the effects of amended train working due to the ongoing Bathampton and Box blockade are apparent, as Platforms 13 and 15 are normally occupied mainly by London trains. In this view No 153325 occupies Platform 13 (centre) as 2A99, the 0706 Gloucester to Bristol Temple Meads service, and No 221128 waits in Platform 15 (right) forming 1V41, the 0642 Birmingham New Street to Paignton service. On the left No 158957 is in Platform 11 working 2D33, the 0748 Bath Spa to Bristol Parkway local.

BRISTOL TEMPLE MEADS: On 26 August 1956 our photographer has walked down to the west end of Platform 3 (now Platform 12) and turned around to take this photograph of No 5971 *Merevale Hall*. Steam traction dominates the scene, together with 1930s signalling and other infrastructure from the steam era.

The present-day view is not so different, as we witness a quiet moment on the morning of 6 February 2019. Two IETs sit in Platforms 13 and 15 and a three-car Class 166 unit, forming a local service, occupies Platform 11. The final (and 57th) Class 800 IET set was accepted by GWR into service on 19 December 2018, the first having entered traffic on 16 October 2017; the nine-car trains entered service in June 2018. A total of 36 Class 802 sets are also on order for West of England services. Modern glass-fronted buildings occupy former industrial sites to the north of the station and on the right the derelict former Post Office building stands empty and awaiting the redevelopers. Note the simplified track layout to the right, now that Bath Road depot is no longer operational.
H. C. Casserley/Tim Maddocks

BRISTOL TEMPLE MEADS: Internally refurbished but still externally in its previous Silverlink livery, No 150121, newly transferred to FGW, waits in Bristol Temple Meads to form the 1042 Gloucester-Weymouth service on Saturday 4 September 2010.

BRISTOL TEMPLE MEADS: In warm spring sunshine, No 150221, coupled to No 150246, pauses in Platform 8 on Tuesday 30 April 2013 forming 2C73, the 1100 Cardiff Central to Taunton local.

BRISTOL TEMPLE MEADS: Working what would have been classed as an 'inter-regional' service in the past, South West Trains unit No 159107 sits in FGW territory as it waits at Platform 12 to form the 1251 departure to Waterloo on Thursday 29 March 2012.

BRISTOL TEMPLE MEADS: Back in the days when the rail system still moved meaningful amounts of Royal Mail traffic, one of the Class 08 diesel shunters was employed to marshall it at Bristol Temple Meads. One such 08 is seen here on 1 April 2001, with a matching brake van. The loco and van are standing on the line that leads to the former Platform 2 bay, which was once used for Portishead trains but at the time was used for parcels traffic. *Phil Marsh*

BATH ROAD SHED: 'Star' Class 4-6-0 No 4056 *Princess Margaret* is stabled on Bath Road shed on 23 April 1954. By this time only three 'Stars' remained in service, and No 4056 would become the last in service, being withdrawn from Bath Road in October 1957. *David Holmes*

BATH ROAD SHED: This classic diesel-hydraulic-era photo of the shed was taken on 14 October 1971. 'Hymek' No D7047 is in the foreground, while a couple of 'Warships' and some diesel-electric interlopers can be seen in the background. Particularly noteworthy is one of the Bristol Pullman sets, the previous pure lines of its Nanking Blue livery arguably now disfigured by the application of the newer grey and blue livery and the presence of jumper cables on the front of the power car. All of the diesel Pullman sets would be withdrawn by 1973. *Tom Heavyside*

BATH ROAD SHED: A few more weeds are now present in this view of the depot on 21 May 1995, with a selection of Class 47s resting on shed. It would eventually close in September of that year.

Oh dear! The present-day view taken on 4 September 2010 reveals that all evidence of railway activity on the site of the locomotive sheds has been removed and the site levelled. There have been a number of plans for the site since the shed was demolished but none have, as yet, come to fruition. The sale and clearance of the site was arguably premature, as there is no doubt that useful, operational railway land in the Bristol area is at a premium, resulting in organisations like Freightliner HeavyHaul having to use a relatively unsatisfactory site at Stoke Gifford, simply because there is now nowhere else left.

BRISTOL TEMPLE MEADS: It's a busy, crowded scene on Wednesday 12 August 2015 as commuters queue to exit the station at the ticket barriers (now known as 'gatelines'). By 2018 some 11.3 million passengers a year were using the station, a number that is set to rise. Accordingly, Network Rail has opened two new 'gateline' entrances to the station to help ease this congestion, one at Queen Anne Gate and the other adjacent to Bonaparte's Cafe, both leading onto Platform 3.

BRISTOL TEMPLE MEADS: A missed opportunity? The original Brunel train shed is seen on 4 September 2010, looking north away from the buffer stops, with the bulk of Bristol Panel squarely blocking any current possibility of it being restored for use. Following the decline in services in the early 1960s, the old station was closed to traffic in September 1965 and subsequently converted to a car park, the same use to which it is now being put, more than 50 years later. During the early stages of rail industry

discussions regarding renewal and enhancements in the Bristol area a few years ago, there was serious talk within Network Rail and FGW concerning the possible reopening of two long platforms within the old train shed as an ideal location for starting and terminating electric services to and from London. FGW considered the close proximity of the old train shed to the main entrance to the station to be a significant selling point for its London customers. With the opportunity to resignal the Bristol area and transfer control to Didcot, the panel building could be removed, thus allowing tracks into the old station again. Yet sadly, the reality has not, as yet, matched the optimism of a few years ago.

BRISTOL TEMPLE MEADS: The elegant lines of the 1874 Digby Wyatt exterior, complete with 100-foot clock tower, are seen on 23 April 2004.

BRISTOL TEMPLE MEADS: The configuration of the station and its railway environs are clear in this aerial view taken on 2 April 2016. The operational station is squarely in the centre of the photo, with the old train shed to the left. Cars are now parked on the site of the former High Level Sidings and two new office blocks occupy part of the site of the old covered goods depot. Bristol East Junction and Barton Hill depot can be seen towards Filton, South Wales and the north curving left.

Index of locations

Past & Present • Mortons Books